Tax Free Retirement Roadmap

CALCULATE
ROTH CONVERSIONS
AVOID TAXES, RMDs &
PROTECT HEIRS

SAVE THOUSANDS ON TAXES & PROTECT YOUR RETIREMENT

Boom Retirement Solutions

Tax Free Retirement Roadmap

A Guide to

Roth Conversions, Avoiding Taxes and RMDs

In Retirement

By Jeff Weidner

Boom Retirement Solutions

Published by Jeff Weidner

Wake Forest, NC

Description:

First Edition

Published in Wake Forest, NC by Boom Retirement Solutions, 2025

Summary:

This guide provides a step-by-step guide on how and when to perform Roth Conversions to reduce or eliminate tax liabilities and Required Minimum Distributions (RMDs), and achieve lasting financial success in retirement.

Author: Jeff Weidner

Dedication

To all those approaching retirement, may you find the confidence and clarity to make the most of your retirement assets, reduce your taxes and create the retirement you deserve.

And to my family, whose support made this book possible.

Acknowledgments
Writing a book about Tax Strategies for Retirees that is both comprehensive and accessible requires the support and expertise of many individuals. I would like to express my deepest gratitude to:

My clients, whose questions and concerns helped shape the content of this book. Your trust in me to guide you through retirement planning decisions has been both a privilege and an inspiration. The team at Boom Retirement Solutions, whose dedication to serving our clients with excellence provides the foundation for everything we do. Your commitment to helping people create secure retirement income strategies makes our work meaningful and impactful.

My mentors in the financial services industry taught me the importance of putting clients first and always continuing to learn. Your guidance has been invaluable in developing the expertise shared in these pages.

The editorial team, whose careful attention to detail helped ensure this complex subject matter is presented clearly and accurately. Your contributions have made this book more accessible and useful for readers.

My family, whose patience and support during the writing process made this book possible. Your encouragement kept me going through long hours of research and writing.

Finally, to you, the reader, for taking this important step toward understanding and maximizing your tax liabilities in retirement. Your commitment to creating a secure retirement future is admirable.

How to Use This Book
This book is designed to be used as a workbook and help you understand and maximize your specific tax strategies to reduce tax liability in retirement. Each chapter builds upon the previous one, providing a comprehensive understanding of the tax system and how it fits into your retirement planning.

Key Features:

Real-World Examples: Throughout the book, you'll find stories of real people facing common retirement tax decisions. These examples illustrate how different strategies can be applied to various situations.

Charts and Tables: Visual aids help clarify complex concepts and provide quick reference for important information.

Action Steps: Each chapter ends with specific steps you can take to apply what you've learned to your own situation.

Worksheets: The workbook and the appendices contain practical worksheets to help you calculate your benefits, analyze your options, and create your retirement income plan, understand conversion thresholds including IRMAA, and RMDs.

Resource Directory: A comprehensive listing of additional resources and contact information is provided to help you access the support you need. Each has links to the specific IRS code and publications that we are referencing for additional information and clarification.

Contents

Pillar 1 — The "Forever Low Taxes" Opportunity

Introduction and Key Points

For years, retirees raced to "beat the 2026 tax cliff." That deadline is gone. With today's lower brackets made permanent under the 2025 tax changes, the game has shifted from panic to planning advantage. This pillar shows you—clearly and calmly—how to use this environment to keep more of your money, cut lifetime taxes, and create more tax-free retirement income. **Use this as a hands-on workbook—complete the short prompts, checklists, and write-in exercises as you go so you finish with a personalized, dollar-specific plan.**

In the next 15 minutes, you'll see why taxes are the silent drag on retirement wealth, how marginal tax rates (the rate on your next dollar) drive smart decisions, and exactly where your opportunity lives. You'll finish with a simple number: the safe amount you can convert or reposition this year without tripping higher brackets or Medicare surcharges.

What you'll do in this module

- Spot your personal "headroom" inside your target tax bracket
- Understand how today's rules open the door for multi-year Roth conversions
- See how small moves now reduce (or erase) future RMDs and Social Security taxation
- Turn the "tax rules" into a one-page opportunity you can act on immediately

What to have handy

- Last year's Form 1040 (and a rough year-to-date income estimate)
- Your filing status (single/married) and current age(s)
- A sense of when you plan to start Social Security and when RMDs will begin

Your outcome

By the end of Pillar 1, you'll complete the **Tax Savings Opportunity Worksheet** and leave with a clear, confidence-building target for this year—and a simple plan to capitalize on the **best tax environment you're likely to see** in retirement.

Key Points:

- **Permanent Tax Rates:** The lower brackets and higher standard deductions from the 2017 TCJA (Tax Cuts and Jobs Act) were set to expire in 2026—but OBBBA One Big Beautiful Bill Act) signed on **July 4, 2025** made them permanent.
- **Higher SALT (State and Local Tax) Deduction:** Cap raised to $40,000 (married) or $20,000 (single) through 2029.
- **Senior Deduction:** New $6,000 deduction for those 65+, phased out at higher incomes.
- **Child Tax Credit Updates:** Raised to $2,200 per child and indexed for inflation.
- **No More "Rush Before 2026" Deadline:** You now have an *open window* to plan Roth conversions and other tax-free strategies under these extended low rates—but waiting could cost you if Congress changes direction in the future.

Why This Matters for Retirees:

- You can now plan **multi-year Roth conversions** without worrying about a tax cliff in 2026.
- The SALT change and senior deduction create **additional levers** for reducing taxable income in retirement.
- Permanence doesn't mean "forever safe"—future Congresses can still alter tax laws, but this is the **best tax environment you're likely to see in your lifetime**.

Action Step:

Use the **Tax Savings Opportunity Worksheet** to:

1. List your current taxable retirement accounts (IRAs, 401(k)s, etc.)
2. Estimate how much tax you'd pay on withdrawals under today's rates
3. Identify potential savings by converting portions to Roth IRAs over the next 3–5 years

The Rationale (a.k.a. "the science" in plain English)

Compounding works both ways.
Money that compounds **tax-free** grows faster than money that must pay a toll (income tax now, or later). Even small frictions—paying 22–24% on conversions or withdrawals, being forced to take **RMDs** in your 70s, or triggering **Medicare IRMAA** surcharges—can snowball over 10–25 years by shrinking what stays invested. Two levers help you fight that drag: (1) shift dollars into **tax-free vehicles** (e.g., Roth), and (2) **reduce future forced income** that would otherwise kick off taxes and surcharges. (See IRS on Roth tax treatment and RMD timing; CMS/SSA on IRMAA mechanics.) **IRS+1 CMS Social Security Administration https://www.irs.gov/retirement-plans/roth-iras?utm_source=chatgpt.com**

Marginal vs. effective tax rate.
Planning is about your **marginal** rate—the tax on your **next** dollar of income—not your average (effective) rate. If your next dollar today is taxed at, say, 22%, and you can move that dollar into a Roth where future qualified withdrawals are **0%**, you've traded a known, lower rate **now** for **none** later. That is why tactics like **"bracket filling"** (converting only up to the top of your target bracket) and **multi-year ladders** often beat one-shot moves: you keep today's marginal rate low while permanently eliminating tax on future growth. (IRS confirms qualified Roth distributions are tax-free and Roths have no lifetime RMDs.)

Why 2025 matters.
In **July 2025**, the **One Big Beautiful Bill Act (H.R. 1, 119th Congress)** became law, **permanently extending** the core individual rate cuts from the 2017 TCJA and adding senior-friendly tweaks that widen planning room. Highlights include:

- **Individual rate extensions** (removing the old "2026 cliff"),
- A new **$6,000 deduction for seniors (65+)** with phaseouts, and
- A higher **SALT cap** (e.g., $40,000 for many joint filers) through 2029.
  Practically, that means you can design **multi-year Roth conversion ladders** and other income-smoothing strategies under friendlier rules, instead of racing a deadline. (See Congress.gov bill record; IRS summaries; and official admin summaries.)

Takeaway.
The old "beat the deadline" mindset is gone; the advantage now is **disciplined planning**: use today's rules to **reposition** dollars into tax-free accounts and **shrink future forced taxable income** (RMDs, IRMAA exposure). The earlier you start, the more years of **tax-free compounding** you capture—and the less room there is for taxes and surcharges to erode your retirement income.

Real-World Example (illustrative)

Snapshot

Pat (63) & Lee (61) — married filing jointly

- **Balances:** $1.1M in Traditional IRA/401(k), $120k in taxable brokerage
- **Income:** No pension; moderate consulting income that ends this year
- **Social Security:** Pat at 67, Lee at 65
- **Goal:** Keep **lifetime taxes** and **Medicare (IRMAA)** surcharges low, build **tax-free** reserves for flexibility and heirs

Planning Assumptions (kept simple for illustration)

- Target top bracket for planning: **22%**
- Stay **below the first IRMAA tier** each year (two-year lookback applies)
- RMD age for both will be **75** (born in 1960+); first-year RMD ≈ **4%** of pre-tax balance (illustrative)
- Legislative landscape provides room for **multi-year conversions** and higher itemized deduction potential (e.g., SALT cap window)

What They Did (5-Year Playbook)

Year 1 (Ages 63 & 61):

- Convert **$90,000** (fills remaining room in 22% bracket).
- "Bunch" giving into a **Donor-Advised Fund (DAF)** to offset part of the added income.
- End-of-year check to confirm IRMAA safety margin.

Year 2 (64 & 62):

- Convert **$90,000** again (repeat bracket-fill).
- If markets dip ≥10–15%, execute an **extra** conversion up to remaining headroom.
- Keep MAGI below the next IRMAA tier.

Year 3 (65 & 63):

- Convert **$100,000** (slightly larger conversion).
- Leverage **senior deduction** now available for Pat (65+) to "squeeze in" more while staying IRMAA-safe.
- Consider modest capital-loss harvesting in taxable to offset other income.

Year 4 (66 & 64):

- Convert **$100,000** again (repeat bracket-fill).
- Lee turns **65** the following year—plan to combine senior deduction + itemized deductions next year if helpful.

Year 5 (67 & 65):

- Convert **$70,000** (final tune-up while Pat starts Social Security).
- Re-run full tax projection with SS included to avoid tipping into a higher IRMAA tier.
- Lock in beneficiary updates on all accounts (primary + contingent).

Total moved to Roth over 5 years:

- $90k + $90k + $100k + $100k + $70k = **$450,000** (computed as 90+90=180; 180+100=280; 280+100=380; 380+70=**450**).

Directional tax paid on conversions (if ~22% average):

- $450,000 × 22% = **$99,000** (45×22=990; add three zeros → **99,000**).
  (This is illustrative; actual brackets, deductions, and credits change the bill.)

Why This Specific Mix?

- **Bracket-filling** avoids jumping to the next tax tier.
- **DAF bunching** turns several years of giving into one large deduction when it matters most.
- **Senior deduction** years let them convert **slightly more** without IRMAA creep.
- A **market-dip trigger** shifts future rebound growth into the Roth (tax-free).

Directional Result (what changes by age 75)

Without any conversions, a first-year RMD (≈4% for illustration) on **$1.1M** would be about:

- **$44,000** (0.04 × 1,100,000 = **44,000**).

After the five-year ladder (ignoring market growth just to show the mechanics), the pre-tax balance is **$1.1M − $450k = $650k**, and a 4% first-year RMD would be about:

- **$26,000** (0.04 × 650,000 = **26,000**).

Directional reduction in forced taxable income at RMD start:

- ~$44,000 −$26,000 = $18,000 per year** (44,000 − 26,000 = **18,000**).
- The ~ symbol means "approximately."
- Why "approximate"? We used a simple 4% RMD factor and ignored market moves and exact IRS table factors for clarity. In reality, the IRS Uniform Lifetime Table at your RMD start age gives a precise divisor (e.g., ~24.7 at 75 → ~4.05%).

That ~$18k/yr less forced income helps:
• keep them **below IRMAA tiers**,
• reduce taxation of **Social Security**, and
• stabilize **net take-home** in retirement.
Meanwhile, the **$450k** in the Roth continues to **compound tax-free**, can be tapped at **0%**, and passes to heirs without creating a big tax spike.

Stress-Test Rules They Added

- **If portfolio falls ≥10–15%** from the recent high, convert up to remaining headroom that year.
- **If unexpected income hits** (sale of a property, big gains), **reduce** that year's conversion to preserve IRMAA safety.
- **Annual November review**: refresh brackets, IRMAA thresholds, SS timing, and charitable plans.

Compliance & Reality Check

- This is an **illustration**, not advice. Exact brackets, IRMAA thresholds, deductions, and investment returns vary.
- Always use current-year numbers and confirm with a qualified tax professional before executing conversions or itemizing strategies.

Step-by-Step Implementation Plan (15 minutes)

Goal: end with a precise **"max safe conversion"** target for this year, a **3–5 year ladder**, and calendar reminders so you actually do it.

Minute 0–2: Gather the essentials

- Last year's **Form 1040** (and any schedules)
- **YTD income** (pay stubs, 1099s, IRA withdrawals)
- Rough **dividends/interest/capital gains** expected this year
- Your **filing status** (single / married filing jointly)
- Your **age(s)** and approximate **Social Security**/RMD start dates

Minute 3–5: Pick your target top bracket

- Decide the **highest bracket** you're willing to touch this year (commonly 22% or 24% for planning).
- Look up (or have software/advisor provide) the **top dollar** of that bracket for your filing status.
- **Write it down** as: Top Of Bracket = ________.

Tip: If you're risk-averse, choose the lower bracket (e.g., 22%) your plan will "fill" but not exceed.

Minute 6–8: Project your taxable income (simple version)
Use quick estimates—perfection isn't required for this pass.

1) Project AGI (Adjusted Gross Income):
AGI = wages/consulting + IRA/401(k) withdrawals + interest + dividends + capital gains + rental/business income + other income − above-the-line deductions (HSA, IRA deduction, etc.)

2) Choose deduction type:
Use **standard** or **itemized** (whichever you expect to be larger).

3) Project taxable income:
Projected Taxable = AGI − (Standard or Itemized Deduction)

Write it down: Projected Taxable = ________.

Minute 9–10: Compute your "headroom"
Headroom = Top Of Bracket - Projected Taxable
That's your **max safe conversion** before you spill into the next bracket.
Mini example (just math):
If Top Of Bracket = 190,000 and Projected Taxable = 155,000 →
Headroom = 190,000 − 155,000 = 35,000.
So your **max safe conversion ≈ $35,000**.
Safety buffer: If your estimates are rough, leave **$2k–$5k** under the line to avoid bracket creep.

Minute 11: IRMAA (Medicare surcharge) check

- IRMAA is based on **MAGI** (AGI + tax-exempt interest) with a **two-year lookback**.
- Compare your **estimated MAGI** to the **current IRMAA tiers** for your filing status.
- If your conversion would push you over a tier, **trim it** so you stay below the threshold—again, leave a small **buffer**.

Quick reminder: This year's MAGI affects your Medicare premiums **two years** later.

Minute 12: Scan for offsets (optional power-ups)
Use deductions/losses you already have—or can create—to **absorb** more conversion without raising net taxes:

- **Charitable bunching / Donor-Advised Fund (DAF):** consolidate several years of giving into one high-deduction year.
- **Capital-loss harvesting (taxable accounts):** realize losses to offset gains and up to $3,000 of ordinary income.
- **HSA contributions** (if eligible): triple-tax advantage.
- **Senior deduction (65+)** if applicable.
- **Higher itemized deductions** (e.g., SALT limit within current rules).

Only use what applies to you. Don't force a strategy that creates other problems.

Minute 13: Draft your 3–5 year playbook

- **Front-load "bridge years"**: bigger conversions in years **after** work ends but **before** Social Security and RMDs start.
- **Market-dip trigger**:
  "If portfolio declines **10–15%** from recent high, convert **up to remaining headroom** that year."
- **Aging milestones**: note when you (a) turn **65** (Medicare & potential senior deduction), (b) plan to **start Social Security**, and (c) hit **RMD age**—your conversion room usually **shrinks** after these.

Minute 14–15: Calendar & communicate

- Add an annual **"Tax-Free Review"** to your calendar for **Nov–Dec** (final true-up when numbers are clearer).
- Add a **mid-year check** (May–June) to adjust for surprises (bonuses, asset sales, big dividends).
- Send a short note to your tax pro/advisor/agent (copy/paste):

Subject: Roth conversion plan - bracket fill & IRMAA safe
Hi [Name],
I'd like to execute a Roth conversion this year that **fills the [22%/24%] bracket** without crossing into the next tier and stays **below the IRMAA threshold** for my filing status.

- My current **Projected Taxable** is about $______.
- The **Top Of Bracket** I'm targeting is $______.

- That gives me **Headroom ≈ $______** for conversion.
  Please confirm these figures with current-year tables, check my IRMAA margin, and propose the exact conversion amount and timing. Also note any offsets (DAF, losses, HSA, senior deduction) we should apply.
  Thanks!

Tax Snapshot

Field	Value
Filing status	___________
Age(s)	___________
Top of bracket (target)	$_____________
AGI (projected)	$_____________
Deduction (std/itemized)	$_____________
Projected taxable income	$_____________
Headroom (max safe conversion)	**Top of Bracket − Projected Taxable = $_____________**

IRMAA & Offsets

Item	Value
MAGI formula	**AGI + tax-exempt interest**
IRMAA threshold	$__________
IRMAA buffer	$__________
Offsets to apply (check all that apply)	☐ DAF ☐ Loss harvesting ☐ HSA ☐ Senior deduction ☐ Other: __________

Timing & Triggers

Item	Value
Bridge years (bigger conversions)	20__ , 20__ , 20__
Market-dip trigger	If portfolio − % → **convert up to $**__________ this year
Annual review (mid-year)	(MM/DD) ______
Annual review (year-end)	(MM/DD) ______
This year's conversion order	$____________ by (date) __________

You're done when you have:

1. a **number** for this year's max safe conversion,
2. a **3–5 year** conversion ladder, and
3. the **reminders** and **email** sent so it actually happens.

Mini Case Story

Marsha (67), retired and single.
She'd always assumed "waiting is safer." After working through this module, she decided to run the numbers instead of relying on gut feel.

Starting snapshot

- **Accounts:** $780,000 in a Traditional IRA; $60,000 brokerage; $40,000 cash
- **Income this year:** $38,000 (consulting + dividends/interest)
- **Social Security:** planning to file at **age 70**
- **RMD age: 73** (so ~6 years away)
- **Goal:** Reduce lifetime taxes and avoid IRMAA surcharges while building a tax-free cushion

What she did (step by step)

1) Picked a target bracket (22%).
She chose to "fill" the **22%** bracket but not cross into the next one.

2) Estimated this year's taxable income.

- Projected **AGI** ≈ $52,000 (consulting + dividends/interest; no big capital gains planned)
- Standard deduction (single) assumed for planning → **Taxable ≈ $52,000 − deduction**
- With the deduction, her **projected taxable income** came out near **$52,000** for quick bracket-fill math (she used a conservative, rounded estimate for simplicity).

3) Calculated headroom.

- She looked up the **top dollar** of the 22% bracket for a single filer (from current-year tables).
- For illustration, say the **top of 22%** is **$100,000** (placeholder for planning).
- **Headroom = Top of bracket − Projected taxable**
    - = 100,000 − 52,000
    - = **48,000**

      So her **max safe conversion** ≈ **$48,000** this year (before touching the next bracket).

Digit-by-digit subtraction:
100,000 − 52,000 = (100 − 52) thousand = 48 thousand → **$48,000**.

4) IRMAA check (two-year lookback).
She compared her **MAGI** (AGI + any tax-exempt interest) *with conversion added* to the **first IRMAA tier** for single filers.

- Result: the $48,000 conversion left **a small buffer** under the tier, so no surcharge risk.
- If she had been too close, she would have trimmed the conversion by a few thousand.

5) Used a small DAF gift to offset taxes.
She contributed **$5,000** to a **Donor-Advised Fund** this year to increase itemized deductions in the same year as the conversion.

6) Set a 3-year ladder.

- **Year 1 (age 67):** Convert **$48,000**
- **Year 2 (age 68):** Target **$45,000** (still 22% bracket, leaving IRMAA buffer)
- **Year 3 (age 69):** Target **$40,000** (tapering down as she approaches Social Security at 70)

She also added a **market-dip trigger**:
"If my portfolio falls **10–15%** from its recent high, I'll convert **up to remaining headroom** that year."

7) Estimated the tax on Year-1 conversion (for cash-flow comfort).

- $48,000 × 22% = **$10,560**
  - Check the math: 48,000 × 22 = 1,056,000; divide by 100 → **10,560**

She planned to **withhold from cash** (not from the converted amount) so **every dollar converted lands in the Roth**.
Before / After (directional, for understanding the mechanics)
Without conversions:

- Pre-tax IRA stays larger into her 70s.
- First-year **RMD at 73** uses a ~4% factor (illustrative).
  - On, say, $780,000 → 0.04 × 780,000 = **$31,200** forced taxable income.

With the 3-year ladder above:

- Total moved to Roth ≈ **$48k + $45k + $40k = $133k**.
  - Sum check: 48 + 45 = 93; 93 + 40 = 133; add three zeros → **$133,000**.
- Ignoring market moves just to show mechanics, the IRA base is smaller by **$133,000** when RMDs begin.

- A 4% first-year RMD on **$780,000 − $133,000 = $647,000** is:
    - 0.04 × 647,000 = **$25,880** (since 647 × 4 = 2,588; add two zeros → 258,800? Careful: multiply 647,000 by 0.04 → move two decimals → 25,880).
- **Directional reduction in forced taxable income:**
    - $31,200 − $25,880 = **$5,320** in **year one** alone.
    - Check: 31,200 − 25,880 = (31,200 − 25,000 = 6,200; 6,200 − 880 = **5,320**).

That smaller RMD helps her stay under IRMAA thresholds and reduces taxation of Social Security, year after year.

Meanwhile, the **$133,000** converted is now in a **Roth**:

- Grows **tax-free**,
- Can be tapped at **0%** during volatile markets, and
- Passes to heirs **tax-free** (still subject to the 10-year rule for non-spouse heirs, but without an income-tax spike).

Why this worked for Marsha

- She **used the 22% bracket deliberately** ("bracket filling") rather than guessing.
- She kept an **IRMAA buffer**, avoiding future premium jumps.
- She **front-loaded** conversions into the **bridge years** (67–69) before Social Security and RMDs compress her room.
- A small **DAF** gift improved the tax trade this year without complicating her plan.

Her 10-minute follow-through checklist

- Confirm current bracket tops and IRMAA tiers
- Set **Year-1 conversion = $48,000** (withholding paid from cash)
- Add **mid-year** and **November** reviews to her calendar
- Send the one-paragraph instruction email to her tax pro to finalize the exact numbers and timing

Net result: fewer future RMDs, flatter taxable income, and a growing **Roth safety cushion** she can use at **0%** when markets get choppy.

Pro Tips, Scripts & Shortcuts

Use these copy-paste snippets and checklists to speed up execution, avoid mistakes, and keep everything organized.

1) Advisor / CPA Email Scripts (pick one)

A. One-paragraph "Bracket Fill + IRMAA Safe" (to CPA or planner)

Subject: Roth conversion plan – bracket fill & IRMAA safe

Hi [Name] — I'd like to model a multi-year Roth conversion that fills the [22%/24%] bracket without crossing into the next tier and stays below the IRMAA threshold for my filing status. Please confirm: • The current top-of-bracket number for my filing status • My projected taxable income and MAGI for this year • A recommended conversion amount (with a small safety buffer) Also, note how the senior deduction (if applicable) and SALT itemizing would affect standard vs. itemized for me. Thanks!

B. "Year-End True-Up" (send in Nov/Dec)

Subject: Year-end Roth conversion true-up

Hi [Name] — Please update my year-to-date income and deductions and confirm how much room I have left in the [22%/24%] bracket and below the IRMAA tier. If I have remaining headroom, I'd like to execute a final conversion of $[amount] before 12/31. Kindly confirm the exact amount, the preferred account to convert from, and withholding guidance.

C. "Market-Dip Trigger" (send any time markets pull back)

Subject: Market dip — conversion trigger

Hi [Name] — With markets down ~[X]%, please check my remaining bracket headroom and confirm a Roth conversion amount up to $[max headroom], keeping me IRMAA-safe. I prefer to convert depressed positions to shift the rebound into the Roth. Please advise on timing and lots to use.

2) Custodian Call Script (to execute the conversion)

Hi, I'd like to do a partial Roth conversion from my Traditional IRA to my Roth IRA. • Amount: $[exact amount] • Positions: [cash / pro-rata / specific fund or shares] • Tax withholding: 0% (I will cover taxes from cash outside the IRA) • Timing: Please process on [date] or at market close today if available • Confirm: I want a written confirmation of the conversion amount and the cost basis/lot details Tip: Converting investments "in-kind" avoids selling/buying spreads and keeps you invested.

3) "Don't shrink the Roth" tax-withholding note

- If possible, **pay conversion taxes from cash outside** your IRA/401(k).
- Withholding from the conversion reduces the amount that lands in Roth (less tax-free growth).
- If you **must** withhold, ask your CPA the smallest safe percentage.

4) Quick Offset Ideas — with practical cues

- **DAF "bunching."** If you give annually, consider bundling 2–3 years of gifts into **one** DAF contribution in a conversion year to increase deductions.
- **Capital-loss harvesting.** In taxable accounts, realize losses to offset gains (and up to **$3,000** of ordinary income per year).
- **Medical expense timing.** Deductible medical expenses are generally those **above 7.5% of AGI**—if you have big procedures, grouping them in a conversion year can help.
- **HSA contributions (if eligible).** Triple tax advantage; consider maxing in conversion years.
- **Charitable QCDs (70½+).** After age 70½, Qualified Charitable Distributions from an IRA can satisfy RMDs (once they begin) **without adding to taxable income**.

Only use what aligns with your situation. Your CPA should confirm how each strategy interacts with your deductions under current rules.

5) IRMAA Safety Buffer Tactic

- Determine your **current IRMAA threshold** for your filing status.
- Keep a **$1,000–$5,000 buffer** below the tier to protect against surprises (dividends, capital gains distributions, etc.).
- Remember: **this year's MAGI → premiums in two years.** Put a note on your calendar.

6) Beneficiary Clean-Up Checklist (5 minutes)

- Verify **primary** and **contingent** beneficiaries on **every** retirement and brokerage account.
- Ensure names, SSNs, and percentages are correct; align with your will/trust.
- For complex needs (minors, special needs, spendthrift), ask your attorney about **trusts** owning **Roth** assets for tax-free distributions with guardrails.
- Re-review after life events (marriage, divorce, birth, death).

7) One-Minute "Spouse/Partner Update" (keeps everyone aligned)
Text/Email template

Quick update: I'm converting $[amount] from the Traditional IRA to Roth this month. This keeps us in the [22%/24%] bracket and below IRMAA. Taxes will be paid from cash so the full amount lands in the Roth. We'll review again in November for a year-end true-up.

8) Simple Spreadsheet Columns (for your 3–5 year ladder)
Create a one-sheet view to avoid analysis paralysis:
Year | Filing Status | Top-of-Bracket ($) | Projected Taxable ($) | Headroom ($) | IRMAA Tier ($) | Buffer ($) | Planned Conversion ($) | Offsets (DAF/Loss/HSA) | Notes (SS/RMD/Medical)
Freeze the header row. Add conditional formatting if "Planned Conversion" would cross the next bracket or IRMAA tier.

9) Annual Automation (so you don't forget)

- **Mid-Year Check (May/June):** refresh income, estimate headroom, adjust plan.
- **Year-End True-Up (Nov/Dec):** finalize conversion amount; execute before **12/31**.
- **Market-Dip Alert:** set a watchlist alert at **−10% / −15%** from a recent high.

10) Documentation to Save (tax time will be easier)

- **Custodian confirmation** of the conversion (date/amount/positions).
- **1099-R** (shows distribution) and **5498** (shows Roth contribution/conversion) at tax time.
- Notes from your CPA showing the **bracket and IRMAA math** used.
- Receipts/acknowledgments for **DAF/QCD** and any **medical** deductions.

11) Two Ultra-Short Scripts (when you're in a hurry)
To CPA:
Please confirm my remaining headroom in the [22%/24%] bracket and below IRMAA, and send an exact Roth conversion dollar amount with a $2k safety buffer.

To Custodian:
Convert $[amount] from Traditional IRA to Roth IRA, in-kind, 0% withholding. Email confirmation today, please.
These tiny systems—scripts, buffers, and calendar nudges—turn a "someday" plan into repeatable action that compounds in your favor.

Action Step

Print this or use the attached document
Fill out the one-page "Tax Savings Opportunity Worksheet." You'll end with a clear dollar amount to convert this year, plus a 3–5 year ladder.

1) Header (who/when)

Field	Value
Name(s)	____________________
Filing status	☐ Single ☐ MFJ
Age(s)	______/ ______
Social Security start (MM/YY)	___/ ___
RMD age	______
State (for state tax)	__________

2) Project this year's income (fast math)
Income & Adjustments

Item	Amount
Wages / Consulting	$________
IRA / 401(k) withdrawals	$________
Interest / Dividends	$________
Capital gains (est.)	$________
Other (rental, business, etc.)	$________
Less: Above-the-line deductions (HSA, IRA, etc.)	− $________
Estimated AGI	$________

IRMAA Calculation

Item	Amount
AGI (from above)	$________
+ Tax-exempt interest	$________
MAGI for IRMAA	$________

3) Choose deduction type

Deductions

Option	Amount
Standard (est.)	$________
Itemized (SALT, charity, medical, etc.)	$________

Taxable Income

Formula	Result
Projected Taxable Income = AGI − (Std/Itemized)	$________

4) Pick your target bracket & compute headroom

Item	Value
Target top bracket	☐ 12% ☐ 22% ☐ 24% ☐ Other: ___%
Top-of-bracket dollar (by filing status)	$________
Headroom (Top-of-bracket − Projected Taxable)	$________
Safety buffer (to avoid spillover)	Reserve $2k–$5k
Max safe conversion *(before buffer)*	$________
Planned conversion	$________

Mini example (just to check your math):

If Top-of-bracket = **$190,000** and Projected Taxable = **$155,000**, then Headroom = **$35,000** (190,000 − 155,000 = 35,000).

5) IRMAA check (two-year lookback)

IRMAA Threshold Check — Inputs

Item	Amount
Filing status Tier 1 threshold	$________
Estimated MAGI (from Step 2)	$________
+ Planned conversion added to MAGI	+ $________

IRMAA Threshold Check — Comparison

Total (MAGI + conversion)	Tier 1 threshold	Buffer to stay under *(aim $1k–$5k)*
$________	$________	$________

If over/too close: **trim** the conversion to maintain your buffer.

6) Offsets you'll use this year (optional power-ups)

Select	Offset	Amount	Details
☐	DAF / charitable bunching	$______	—
☐	Capital-loss harvesting (taxable)	$______	Offsets ordinary income up to $3,000
☐	HSA contribution	$______	If eligible
☐	Medical expenses timed this year	$______	Only amounts over 7.5% of AGI
☐	Senior deduction (65+) / other	$______	—

Notes

____

7) Your 3–5 year conversion ladder

Year	Bridge year? (post-work, pre-SS/RMD)	Target bracket	Planned conversion	IRMAA buffer kept?	Notes (DAF, losses, SS/RMD)
20__	☐ Yes ☐ No	___%	$________	☐ Yes ☐ No	______________________
20__	☐ Yes ☐ No	___%	$________	☐ Yes ☐ No	______________________
20__	☐ Yes ☐ No	___%	$________	☐ Yes ☐ No	______________________
20__	☐ Yes ☐ No	___%	$________	☐ Yes ☐ No	______________________
20__	☐ Yes ☐ No	___%	$________	☐ Yes ☐ No	______________________

Market-dip trigger:
"If portfolio declines __% from recent high, convert **up to remaining headroom** that year."

8) Beneficiary quick check (2 minutes)

Item	Selection	Action / Notes
Primary beneficiary(ies) up to date?	☐ Yes ☐ No	–
Contingent beneficiary(ies) listed?	☐ Yes ☐ No	–
Complex needs (minors/special needs/spendthrift)?	☐ Yes ☐ No	If Yes, consider trust review

9) Calendar & Coordination

Item	Status / Date	Notes
Mid-year review	__ /___/20___	
Year-end true-up (Nov–Dec)	__ /___/20___	
Send advisor email (paste your numbers)	__ /___/20___	☐ Done
Custodian script ready	☐ Yes ☐ No	Amount / In-kind / 0% withholding

10) Final Box (Execution Plan)

Item	Value
This year's conversion amount	$________
Fund taxes from	☐ Cash (preferred) ☐ Withholding (%) ____
Execution date window	__ /___/20___ to __ /___/20___
Success criteria	Stay in % bracket and below IRMAA Tier ___ with $____ buffer

Common pitfalls (quick scan)

- ☐ Forgetting mutual-fund **capital-gains distributions** in Dec.
- ☐ Withholding taxes **from** the conversion (shrinks what hits the Roth).
- ☐ Ignoring **state income tax** impact.
- ☐ Taking a conversion **after** RMD starts without satisfying the RMD first.
- ☐ Missing the **two-year IRMAA lookback**.

Fill this page, copy your key numbers into the advisor email, and you've got a concrete plan: **a safe conversion dollar amount for this year** and a **repeatable ladder** for the next 3–5 years.

Summary of Pillar 1

Pillar 1 — Summary
What you learned (key takeaways)

- Today's rules create a **planning advantage**: lower brackets + friendlier deductions mean you can design **multi-year, bracket-aware Roth conversions** instead of racing a deadline.
- Focus on your **marginal rate** (tax on the next dollar), not your average rate. Use **bracket filling** to convert up to (not past) your target bracket.

- Shrinking pre-tax balances before RMD age reduces **forced taxable income**, lowers **IRMAA** risk, and preserves more **tax-free growth** in Roth.
- Smart timing (bridge years, market dips) and **offsets** (DAF bunching, loss harvesting, HSA, senior deduction) improve the trade.

What you did (deliverables from this pillar)

- Completed the **Tax Savings Opportunity Worksheet** with:
  - Filing status, **top-of-bracket** dollar, **projected taxable income, IRMAA tier**, and **this year's safe conversion amount** (with a buffer).
- Built a **3–5 year conversion ladder** (front-loaded into bridge years) and added a **market-dip trigger**.
- Set **calendar reviews** (mid-year + Nov/Dec true-up).
- Prepped the **advisor email** and **custodian script** so execution is quick.
- Verified **primary + contingent beneficiaries** so future Roth dollars transfer cleanly.

How it plays out (from the examples)

- **Pat & Lee:** A 5-year ladder reduced projected first-year RMDs and IRMAA exposure while moving hundreds of thousands into Roth.
- **Marsha:** A precise **$48k** conversion kept her in the target bracket and under IRMAA, cut future RMDs, and created a Roth cushion she can tap at **0%** during volatility.

Common pitfalls to avoid

- Estimating without a **safety buffer** and accidentally crossing the bracket or IRMAA tier.
- **Withholding taxes from the conversion** instead of paying from cash (shrinks what lands in Roth).
- Ignoring **year-end capital-gain distributions** in taxable accounts.
- Forgetting RMD sequencing (once RMDs start, you must take the RMD **before** converting).
- Skipping **state tax** and deduction interactions when you itemize (SALT, charity, medical).

Your next move

- Execute this year's **planned conversion amount** (in-kind if possible, 0% withholding).
- Send the **year-end true-up** note to your CPA in November to finalize.
- Move to **Pillar 2 — Roth Conversion Made Simple** to confirm eligibility nuances, mechanics, and the exact "how-to" for converting cleanly.

Pillar 2 — Roth Conversion Made Simple

Introduction and Key Points

A Roth conversion is a straightforward trade: **pay tax on some pre-tax money now** so it can **grow and be withdrawn tax-free later**—with **no RMDs** on the Roth. This pillar strips out the jargon and shows you, in plain English, **whether a conversion makes sense for you, how much, and when**.

What you'll do in this module

- Get a clear, 2-minute definition of a Roth conversion (IRA/401(k) → Roth IRA or in-plan Roth).
- Learn the moving parts that matter: **marginal tax bracket, IRMAA, bracket-filling, pro-rata rule, Form 8606 basis, five-year rules**, and the "no recharacterization" rule (conversions can't be undone).
- See when conversions shine (bridge years, market dips, legacy planning) and when to **pass** (high-income year, close to an IRMAA cliff, big capital gains, or no cash for taxes).
- Use a quick **Readiness Quiz** to decide: **No Conversion / One-Time Amount / Multi-Year Ladder**.

What to have handy

- Last year's **Form 1040** and year-to-date income.
- **Account balances** by type (Traditional IRA/401(k), Roth, taxable brokerage).
- Any **after-tax (non-deductible) IRA basis** (Form 8606, if applicable).
- Your **estimated tax bracket** and a rough IRMAA tier check.
- When you plan to start **Social Security** and your **RMD age**.

Key cautions (so you don't stub your toe)

- **Withholding:** If possible, pay the tax from **cash outside** the IRA so every converted dollar lands in the Roth.
- **Pro-rata rule:** If you have both pre-tax and after-tax dollars in IRAs, conversions are **pro-rated** across all IRAs.
- **Five-year rules:**
    - For **earnings** to be tax-free, you need a Roth IRA open at least **5 tax years** and be **59½+** (or meet another qualifying event).

    - For **converted principal**, the 10% penalty can apply if withdrawn within 5 years **and** you're under 59½ (less relevant if you're 60+).
- **No do-overs:** Conversion **recharacterization isn't allowed**—double-check your numbers before you pull the trigger.

Your outcome
By the end of Pillar 2 you'll have a **Roth Conversion Readiness Score**, a recommended **conversion path (none / one-time / ladder)**, and a **precise target amount** for your next step—fully aligned with your tax bracket and IRMAA safety buffer.

Key Points:

- **What It Is:** A Roth conversion moves money from a pre-tax retirement account (like a Traditional IRA or 401(k)) into a Roth IRA, triggering income taxes now but eliminating taxes on future growth and withdrawals.
- **Permanent Tax Advantage:** With TCJA's lower tax rates locked in by the **2025 One Big Beautiful Bill Act**, you can spread conversions over multiple years without a looming 2026 tax hike deadline.
- **Flexibility:** You can convert all at once or in smaller amounts over several years ("ladder" strategy) to control your tax bracket.
- **Tax-Free Growth:** Once inside a Roth IRA, your money grows tax-free, and qualified withdrawals are tax-free for you and your heirs.
- **No RMDs:** Roth IRAs are not subject to Required Minimum Distributions, giving you more control over your retirement income.

Why This Matters for Retirees:

- **Protects Against Future Tax Hikes:** Even though rates are "permanent" now, Congress can raise taxes in the future—locking in tax-free income now is a hedge against that risk.
- **Reduces Lifetime Taxes:** A well-planned conversion can save six figures in taxes over your retirement.
- **Estate Planning Benefits:** Passing Roth assets to heirs keeps them from facing a large tax bill on inherited retirement accounts.
- **More Income Control:** Without RMDs, you can choose when and how to take withdrawals, which helps manage Medicare premiums and Social Security taxation.

Action Step:
Complete the **Roth Conversion Readiness Quiz** to:

1. Identify if you're a good candidate for a conversion.
2. Determine the optimal tax bracket for your situation.
3. Decide if you should convert in one lump sum or over several years.

The Rationale (the "why" in plain English)

1) Tax arbitrage you control

- **Plain English:** A Roth conversion lets you *choose* to pay tax at a **known** rate today so that future growth and withdrawals are **0%** (if qualified). If today's **marginal** rate (the tax on your next dollar) is ≤ the rate you or your heirs would pay later, you usually come out ahead.
- **Mini-math:**

Metric	**Roth (convert now)**	**Pre-tax (leave pre-tax)**
Amount considered now	**$50,000 (converted)**	**$50,000 (not converted)**
Current marginal tax rate	**22%**	**–**
Tax paid now	**$11,000** ***(50,000 × 0.22)***	**$0**
Future value at withdrawal	**$100,000**	**$100,000**
Tax rate at withdrawal	**0%**	**24%**
Tax owed at withdrawal	**$0**	**$24,000** ***(100,000 × 0.24)***
Net after-tax withdrawal	**$100,000**	**$76,000**
Directional edge (tax later − tax now)	**$13,000 saved** ***(24,000 − 11,000)***	

When it helps most: In "bridge years" (post-work, pre-SS/RMD) or any year your income dips.

2) Optionality beats precision

- **Plain English:** Roth dollars are **flexible**. In down markets, you can tap Roth at **0%** and avoid selling taxable or pre-tax assets at a loss. In up markets, you can leave Roth alone to compound. That **choice** often beats squeezing every last decimal of "optimal."

- **Why it matters:** Optionality reduces "sequence-of-returns" risk (bad returns early in retirement). Having a **tax-free** bucket gives you a shock absorber during volatility.
- **Planning cue:** Build a **multi-bucket** approach (Roth / pre-tax / taxable). Use the bucket that keeps you under bracket and IRMAA thresholds *this year*.

3) RMD and IRMAA pressure

- **Plain English:** Big pre-tax balances force **RMDs** in your 70s—taxable income whether you need it or not. More income can:
  - push you into **higher tax brackets**,
  - trigger **IRMAA** surcharges on Medicare (based on MAGI with a two-year lookback), and
  - increase how much of your **Social Security** is taxed.
- **Why Roth helps:** Roth IRAs have **no lifetime RMDs**. Converting now shrinks future pre-tax balances, which **reduces forced income** later and helps you stay **below** IRMAA tiers.
- **Rule of thumb:** A smaller pre-tax pile = smaller RMDs = fewer surprise jumps in taxes and Medicare premiums.

4) Estate planning advantage

- **Plain English:** Most non-spouse heirs must empty inherited IRAs within **10 years** (the "10-year rule"). If they inherit **pre-tax** money during peak earning years, those withdrawals stack on top of their salary and can spike their tax bill. If they inherit **Roth**, withdrawals are generally **tax-free** (still within 10 years), avoiding that income-tax surge.
- **Why it matters:** Conversions you do now can **prevent** your kids from paying high marginal rates later on your retirement money.
- **Practical tip:** Keep **beneficiary designations** updated (primary + contingent). For complex needs (minors, special needs, spendthrift), consider trust structures that hold **Roth** assets.

Bottom line: Conversions trade **today's known rate** for **permanent 0% on qualified future withdrawals**, add **flexibility** during market swings, **shrink RMD/IRMAA pressure**, and can **protect heirs** from big tax spikes. When you can convert within your target bracket **and** stay under IRMAA, the math and the lifestyle benefits often align.

Readiness Quiz (score yourself quickly)

How to use this: Read each item. If it's true for you **this year**, give yourself **1 point**. Total your score, then follow the guidance below.

1) I'm in (or can stay in) the 22%–24% bracket with a conversion this year.

- **How to check:** From Pillar 1, use your *Top-of-Bracket* and *Projected Taxable Income* to compute **Headroom**.
- **Say "Yes" if:** You have **> $5k** headroom after leaving a small buffer ($2k–$5k).
- **Why it matters:** You're converting at a reasonable, known rate now instead of risking higher rates later.

2) I'm below the next IRMAA tier with the conversion (with a buffer).

- **How to check:** Estimate **MAGI** (AGI + tax-exempt interest) **plus** your planned conversion; compare to the current IRMAA tier for your filing status.
- **Say "Yes" if:** You'll stay **$1k–$5k under** the next tier.
- **Why it matters:** IRMAA has a **two-year lookback**; avoid surprise premium jumps.

3) I have cash outside retirement accounts to pay the tax (so 100% lands in Roth).

- **How to check:** Multiply planned conversion by your marginal rate (e.g., $40k × 22% = **$8,800** tax).
- **Say "Yes" if:** You can pay that from **cash** (not withholding from the conversion).
- **Why it matters:** Withholding shrinks what reaches the Roth and its future tax-free growth.

4) I'm in bridge years (post-work, pre-RMD/SS) or expect lower income this year.

- **How to check:** Are you retired or semi-retired, not yet taking SS, and pre-RMD? Or did your income drop this year?
- **Say "Yes" if:** You have 1–5 relatively low-income years to "harvest" conversions.
- **Why it matters:** These years usually offer the **cheapest** conversion rates.

5) I want to reduce RMDs and/or leave tax-free assets to heirs.

- **Say "Yes" if:** Smaller RMDs, lower lifetime taxes, or cleaner inheritance are priorities.
- **Why it matters:** Conversions shrink future forced income and create tax-free legacy buckets.

6) My plan/account allows clean mechanics (in-plan Roth or IRA custodian supports in-kind conversions).

- **How to check:** Ask your custodian/plan about **in-kind conversions** and fees; confirm forms (1099-R, 5498) will be issued.
- **Say "Yes" if:** Execution is straightforward and low-friction.
- **Why it matters:** Easy mechanics reduce errors, delays, and trading costs.

7) I'm comfortable holding the conversion long-term (no "undo" after conversion).

- **How to check:** Conversions **can't be recharacterized**. Are you okay riding market ups/downs with those Roth dollars?
- **Say "Yes" if:** You won't need to reverse it or spend the converted funds immediately.
- **Why it matters:** Conversions reward **time in Roth**, not timing.

Score & Next Steps

0–2 points → "Wait or Micro-Test"

- **What to do:** Revisit in 6–12 months. If curious, do a **$5k–$10k test conversion** to learn the mechanics.
- **How to improve your score:**
  - Build cash reserves for taxes (aim for **tax × 1.2** as a cushion).
  - Plan for **bridge years** (delay SS, smooth income).
  - Explore plan options to allow **in-kind** or **in-plan** conversions.

3–5 points → "Partial Conversion (Bracket-Fill)"

- **What to do:** Convert **up to headroom** in your target bracket **with a buffer**.
- **Watchouts:** Keep **IRMAA buffer**, avoid year-end capital-gain surprises, pay tax from cash.
- **Pro tip:** Add a **market-dip trigger** (−10%/−15%) to opportunistically top off.

6–7 points → "Multi-Year Ladder"

- **What to do:** Build a **3–5 year conversion ladder** front-loaded into **bridge years**; true-up each November.
- **Refinements:** Consider **DAF bunching**, **loss harvesting**, **HSA** contributions, and **basis isolation** (if you have after-tax IRA dollars).

Tie-Breakers (when you're on the fence)

- **High state income tax?** Favor **smaller, steadier** annual conversions; consider timing if you might relocate to a **lower-tax** state.
- **Near an IRMAA cliff?** Trim conversion to keep a **$2k–$5k** buffer.
- **Have IRA basis (Form 8606)?** Explore **isolating basis** (roll pre-tax to 401(k) if plan allows) before converting.
- **Large capital-gain event this year?** Downshift or **wait** until next year.
- **Charitable giver? Bunch** gifts (DAF) in a conversion year to offset income.
- **Under 59½?** Mind the **5-year conversion penalty clock** (less relevant at 60+, but note it).

Quick Examples

- **Score 2 (Wait/Test):** Income high, IRMAA tight, no cash for taxes → do a **$5k** test only.
- **Score 4 (Partial):** Bridge year, $30k headroom, cash on hand → convert **$25k–$28k** (leave buffer).
- **Score 7 (Ladder):** Retired, delayed SS, wide IRMAA room, cash for tax → plan **$40k–$60k/yr** for 4 years with year-end true-ups.

Bottom line: Your score isn't about perfection—it's a **go/no-go** confidence check. If you're in the **3–7** range, you likely benefit from **some** conversion this year; size it to your bracket and IRMAA buffer, then execute cleanly.

Key Mechanics (what trips people up)

Use these mini-checklists and examples to avoid the most common missteps.

1) Pro-rata rule (IRAs)
What it means: For tax purposes, **all** of your Traditional/SEP/SIMPLE IRAs are treated as **one** account on **December 31** of the conversion year. If you have any after-tax **basis** (tracked on **Form 8606**), each conversion is part taxable / part nontaxable **in proportion** to your basis.

Quick formula:

- **Nontaxable portion** = Conversion × (IRA **basis** ÷ **year-end total** of all Traditional/SEP/SIMPLE IRAs)
- **Taxable portion** = Conversion − Nontaxable portion

Example: Total IRAs = **$250,000**, basis = **$25,000** (10%). Convert **$40,000** → 10% nontaxable (**$4,000**), **$36,000** taxable.

How to improve the math:

- If your 401(k) accepts **roll-ins**, roll **pre-tax** IRA dollars **into** the 401(k) first. That can **"isolate basis"** in the IRA, then convert the basis with little/no tax.
- Watch the **SIMPLE IRA 2-year rule** (no rollovers out within 2 years of first SIMPLE contribution).

Do this: Find your **Form 8606** history; list **all** IRA balances as of **12/31**; consider a **pre-conversion roll-in** to a plan to isolate basis.

2) Five-year clocks (there are two)

A) Roth IRA "owner" clock (for earnings to be tax-free)

- Starts **Jan 1** of the year you first **fund any Roth IRA** (contribution or conversion).
- Once this clock shows **5 tax years and** you're **59½+**, **earnings** are tax-free on qualified distributions.

  Pro tip: Open a small Roth IRA **now** (even $100) to start/keep this clock running.

B) Converted principal clock (early-withdrawal penalty test)

- Each **conversion** has its **own** 5-year clock.
- If you're **under 59½**, withdrawing converted principal within 5 years can trigger the **10% penalty** (tax on earnings still depends on the owner clock).
- For most ages **60+**, this is **moot**, but good to know.

Ordering rules (useful if you take money out):

1. **Roth contributions** come out first (tax/penalty-free),
2. then **conversion basis** (older conversions first),
3. then **earnings** last.

3) No recharacterization (no "undo")

What it means: Since 2018, **Roth conversions cannot be recharacterized**. Once you convert, you can't reverse it.

Implication: Double-check **amount**, **IRMAA buffer**, and **timing**. Many people leave a **$2k–$5k** safety gap.

4) RMD sequencing (critical once RMDs start)

Rule: In an RMD year, you **must take the IRA's RMD first**. The RMD itself **cannot** be converted. Only **amounts above** the RMD are eligible for conversion.

Example: RMD = **$18,000**. You want to convert **$30,000**. You must first **distribute $18,000** (taxable), then you **may convert up to $30,000** more.

Note: The **still-working exception** can delay RMDs from your **current employer's** plan (if you don't own >5%), but not from **IRAs**.

5) State taxes & withholding
Why it matters: Some states tax conversions; some don't. Withholding **from the conversion** reduces what reaches the Roth.
Best practice: Set **0% withholding** on the conversion and pay the tax from **cash** (or do a small **estimated tax** payment).
Penalty safety: To avoid underpayment penalties, use the IRS **safe harbor** (e.g., pay 100%/110% of last year's tax via estimates/withholding) or increase W-2 withholding late in the year (withholding is treated as paid evenly all year).

6) 401(k)/403(b) plan nuances
In-plan Roth conversion (IRR): Many plans let you convert **pre-tax** balances to **Roth 401(k)** internally. Different **five-year** rules can apply inside plans.
Roll-ins to plans: Rolling **pre-tax IRA** funds into a 401(k) can **remove** them from the IRA aggregation rule—handy for **isolating basis**.
Check first: Investment options, fees, Roth distribution rules, and whether your plan accepts roll-ins.
After-tax in plans: Some plans allow **after-tax (non-Roth)** contributions → **in-plan** or **to Roth IRA** (the "mega backdoor" path). Not needed for most, but powerful if available.

7) Paperwork & proof (don't skip)

- **1099-R**: Issued by the distributing account (shows the distribution/conversion).
- **5498**: Issued by the Roth custodian (shows Roth contributions/conversions received).
- **Form 8606**: Tracks **IRA basis** and computes the taxable/nontaxable share of conversions.
- **Keep**: Custodian confirmations, year-end balances (for pro-rata), and your CPA's bracket/IRMAA math.

8) Quick "green-light" checklist (before you hit Convert)

- ☐ **Headroom** confirmed (target bracket) with **$2k–$5k buffer**
- ☐ **IRMAA tier** safe with **$1k–$5k buffer**
- ☐ **Basis / 8606** reviewed; roll-in done if isolating basis
- ☐ **State tax** impact checked; plan for **0% withholding** + cash for tax
- ☐ **RMD** handled first (if applicable)
- ☐ **Custodian/plan** can do **in-kind** conversion; fees acceptable
- ☐ **Paperwork** steps clear (1099-R, 5498, 8606) and saved to your tax folder

Nail these mechanics once, and every future conversion becomes a fast, low-stress repeat.

Step-by-Step Implementation (10–15 minutes)

Goal: end with a **specific, scheduled conversion amount**, clean mechanics, and zero surprises on taxes or IRMAA.

Minute 0–2 — Confirm your lane (import from Pillar 1)

Write these at the top of your worksheet:

Field	Value
Target bracket	____%
Top-of-bracket $	**$________**
Projected taxable income	**$________**
Headroom (Top-of-bracket − Projected taxable)	**$________**
IRMAA buffer (stay $1k–$5k under next tier)	**$________ room**
Reminder	**If anything changed since Pillar 1 (bonus, property sale, big dividends), re-run the Pillar-1 math first.**

Minute 3–4 — Check for basis (Form 8606)

- Find your last **Form 8606**. **Basis?** ☐ Yes ☐ No
- If **Yes**, consider **isolating basis** before converting:
  1. Ask your 401(k)/403(b) if they accept **roll-ins** of **pre-tax IRA** dollars.
  2. If allowed, roll **pre-tax** IRA funds into the plan → leaves **after-tax basis** in the IRA.
  3. Convert the **remaining basis** to Roth (little/no tax).
- Note **all IRA balances as of 12/31** matter for the **pro-rata** calculation.

Mini example: IRAs total $250k with $25k basis (10%). Convert $40k → $4k nontaxable / $36k taxable unless you isolate basis first.

Minute 5–6 — Choose the account & lots

- **Source:** ☐ Traditional IRA ☐ 401(k)/403(b) (in-plan Roth conversion)
- **Method:** Prefer **in-kind** (move the actual shares) so you stay invested.
- **What to move:** Depressed positions are fine—future rebound compounds **tax-free** in Roth.
- **Fees/lockups:** Check trading windows, short-term redemption fees (funds/ETFs), and plan fees.

Minute 7–8 — Pick the amount (use your headroom)

- Start with **Headroom** from Minute 0–2.
- Subtract a **safety buffer** of **$2k–$5k** (bracket/IRMAA wiggle room).
- **Planned conversion = Headroom − Buffer = $________**
- Quick **IRMAA check:** MAGI (AGI + tax-exempt interest) + conversion stays **below tier − buffer**? ☐ Yes

Micro-example: Headroom $35,000; buffer $3,000 → plan **$32,000** conversion.

Minute 9–10 — Line up the tax (pay from cash)

- Estimate federal tax: **Conversion × marginal rate** (e.g., $32,000 × 22% = **$7,040**).
- Add state estimate if applicable.
- Fund taxes from **cash** (savings, taxable account)—set **0% withholding** on the conversion so **100%** lands in Roth.
- **Penalty safety:** If you're worried about underpayment penalties, either:
    - hit the IRS **safe harbor** (pay 100%/110% of last year's tax), **or**
    - increase W-2 withholding late in the year (treated as paid evenly all year), **or**
    - make/adjust **estimated payments**.

Minute 11–12 — Execute with custodian/plan

Webform / call checklist:

- From: **Traditional IRA/401(k)** → To: **Roth IRA/Roth 401(k)**
- **Amount:** $________
- **Positions:** ☐ In-kind (list funds/ETFs/stocks) ☐ Cash
- **Tax withholding: 0%** (I'll pay from cash)
- **Timing:** Process on __ /___/20___ (or "at market close today")
- **Confirm:** "Email me written confirmation of date, amount, and positions transferred."

Script:
"Please convert **$[amount]** from my Traditional IRA to my Roth IRA **in-kind** with **0% withholding**. Send written confirmation of the exact amount, date, and positions. Thank you."

Minute 13 — Document

- Save **custodian confirmation** (PDF).
- Track in your spreadsheet: amount, date, positions, headroom used, IRMAA buffer left.
- Create a tax folder for:
  - **1099-R** (distribution) — arrives after year-end
  - **5498** (Roth funding/conversion) — arrives after year-end
  - **Form 8606** (basis / conversion reporting)

Minute 14–15 — Review in Nov/Dec (true-up window)

- Ask CPA: "How much **headroom** remains under my target bracket & IRMAA tier?"
- If safe, do a **small top-off** conversion before **12/31**.
- Watch for **capital-gains distributions** (taxable funds often pay in Dec)—recheck headroom if they hit.

Year-end email (copy/paste):
"Please update my YTD income and confirm remaining room in the **[22%/24%]** bracket and below the **IRMAA** tier. If I have safe headroom, I'd like to convert **$[amount]** before 12/31 with **0% withholding**."

"Done" Checklist (print this)

- ☐ Headroom & IRMAA buffer confirmed (with $2k–$5k cushion)
- ☐ Basis/8606 reviewed; roll-in done if isolating basis
- ☐ Amount chosen and taxes funded from **cash**
- ☐ Conversion executed **in-kind** with **0% withholding**
- ☐ Confirmation saved; tax docs queued (1099-R, 5498, 8606)
- ☐ **Nov/Dec** true-up on calendar; custodian/CPA emails drafted

Nail this once and every future conversion becomes a 10-minute rinse-and-repeat.

Real-World Examples (short & practical)

Numbers are illustrative to show the mechanics. Always use your actual bracket tops, IRMAA tiers, and current-year projections.

1) Clean IRA (no basis), bridge year — Kim (62)

- **Snapshot:** Retired this spring; no Social Security yet; Traditional IRA balance healthy; taxable income modest.
- **Lane (from Pillar 1):** Headroom in the **22%** bracket = **$42k**; IRMAA buffer ≈ **$3k**.
- **Action:**
  - Converts **$40,000** now (leaves a ~$2k safety buffer).
  - Pays tax from cash: **$40,000 × 22% = $8,800** federal (plus any state).
  - Adds a **market-dip trigger**: if the S&P 500 falls **≥12%**, convert **up to $10,000** more (so long as headroom remains and IRMAA safe).
- **Why it works:** Classic **bridge year**—low income, wide headroom, no IRMAA risk.
- **Outcome:** Smaller future RMD base; Roth grows tax-free; optional year-end **true-up** if headroom remains.

2) With basis, wants isolation — Carlos (64)

- **Snapshot:** Traditional IRA **$150,000** with **$20,000** after-tax basis (tracked on **Form 8606**).
- **Problem:** Pro-rata rule would make most of any conversion **taxable** unless he isolates basis.
- **Action (two steps):**
  1. His 401(k) **accepts roll-ins**, so he rolls **$130,000 pre-tax** from his IRA **into the 401(k)** (leaving only the **$20,000 basis** in the IRA).
  2. Converts the remaining **$20,000** IRA basis to Roth—**minimal tax** because nearly all of it is after-tax dollars.
- **Why it works:** Rolling pre-tax dollars **out** of the IRA removes them from the **year-end aggregation pool**, effectively **isolating basis** before converting.
- **Outcome:** Roth funded at low tax cost; future RMD base reduced by $20k; keeps 401(k) invested pre-tax for later planning.

3) High-income year — skip now, go bigger later — Priya (67)

- **Snapshot:** Sold a rental this year; **MAGI** already close to the next **IRMAA** tier; starting Social Security next year.
- **Risk:** Any conversion now could **tip IRMAA** (two-year lookback) and push capital gains into a higher bracket.

- **Action:**
  - **Wait** this year (or do a token **$5k test** to learn mechanics only).
  - Build next year's plan: fill the **22%** bracket with **$45k–$55k** (leaving a buffer), coordinate with charitable **DAF bunching** to offset part of the conversion, and monitor capital-gain distributions in December.
- **Why it works:** Avoids compounding a **high-income year** with conversion income; sets up a cleaner, larger conversion when income normalizes.
- **Outcome:** Preserves IRMAA status now; executes a **larger, smarter** conversion next year without premium shocks.

4) In-plan Roth conversion while working — Dana (66)

- **Snapshot:** Still employed; contributing **pre-tax** to 401(k) to keep current taxes reasonable. Plan allows **in-plan Roth conversion (IRR)**.
- **Lane:** Pillar-1 headroom indicates **$27k** in the 22% bracket with IRMAA buffer intact.
- **Action:**
  - Executes an **in-plan Roth conversion** of **$25,000** (leaves buffer).
  - Pays estimated tax from cash (approx. **$25,000 × 22% = $5,500**).
  - Continues **pre-tax** salary deferrals to balance today vs. tomorrow.
- **Nuances:** In-plan Roths have their **own** distribution and five-year rules—she confirms plan specifics and fees.
- **Outcome:** Begins building a **Roth bucket** without rolling funds out of the plan; keeps current-year tax in check; reduces future RMD exposure.

Quick guardrails for all four

- Leave a **$2k–$5k** buffer under your target bracket **and** IRMAA tier.
- Prefer **in-kind** conversions and **0% withholding** (pay tax from cash).
- Set **Nov/Dec** true-up to catch extra headroom (but watch for **fund distributions** in taxable accounts).
- Save **custodian confirmations**; expect **1099-R**, **5498**, and update **Form 8606** if basis applies.

Mini Case Story (narrative)

Ray (68) & Dana (66) — married filing jointly

- **Snapshot:** Ray already started Social Security; Dana will file at 68. They're retired, want more **tax-free flexibility** and to keep **Medicare (IRMAA)** premiums stable.
- **Accounts (illustrative):** $980k in Traditional IRAs/401(k)s, $160k taxable, $50k cash reserve.

- **Goal:** Move steady chunks to **Roth** without tripping a higher tax bracket or an IRMAA tier.

1) Lane check (from Pillar 1)

- **Target bracket:** 22%
- **Headroom this year: $55,000**
- **IRMAA buffer: ~$3,000** under the next tier (two-year lookback). They agree to **leave a cushion** and not use every last dollar of headroom.

2) Conversion plan (why $50k, not $55k)

- **Planned conversion: $50,000** (keeps ~$5k headroom for safety and any surprise income).
- **Tax funding:** From **cash**, not withheld from the conversion.
  - **Federal estimate:** $50,000 × 22% = **$11,000** (plus any state tax).
- **Method: In-kind** — they move ETF/fund shares directly from Traditional IRA to Roth IRA, staying invested and shifting future growth to **0%**.

IRMAA note: The conversion **does** increase MAGI; their CPA confirms they still remain **below** the next IRMAA tier by about **$3k** after the $50k is added.

3) Charitable bunching (helps taxes, not IRMAA)

- They "bunch" **$8,000** of charitable giving into a **Donor-Advised Fund (DAF)** this year to improve **itemized deductions**.
- **Important:** The DAF reduces **taxable income**, but it **does not** reduce **MAGI** (so it doesn't help IRMAA). They already verified IRMAA safety **before** deciding on the DAF.

4) Execution details (clean mechanics)

- **Custodian instructions:** "Convert $50,000 **in-kind** with **0% withholding**; email written confirmation showing date, amount, and positions."
- **Documentation saved:** Custodian confirmation now; expect **1099-R** (distribution) and **5498** (Roth funding) after year-end.
- **Form 8606:** Filed with taxes to report the Roth conversion (even if they have **no IRA basis**).

5) November true-up (top-off safely)

- Year-to-date income lands **slightly below** projections; CPA shows **~$4,000** of safe headroom left in the 22% bracket **with** the IRMAA buffer intact.
- They do a **$4,000 top-off conversion**, again **in-kind, 0% withholding**.

6) Directional impact (what changes and why it matters)

- **Smaller future RMDs:** Every dollar moved from pre-tax to Roth **reduces** the base used to compute RMDs when they hit **age 73** (both are 1950s birth years). Converting **$54,000** this year alone trims the eventual first-year RMD by roughly **~$2,000** (assuming a ~4% factor), and that effect **compounds** if they repeat annually.
- **No IRMAA jump:** Because they left buffers, the two-year lookback won't push premiums up.
- **More tax-free flexibility:** The new Roth dollars can be tapped at **0%** during a market drawdown, helping them manage **sequence-of-returns risk** and keep taxable income steady.
- **Legacy:** Roth growth now accrues **tax-free** for heirs (still generally subject to the 10-year rule, but without the big income-tax spike).

7) Their one-page recap (what they actually did)

- Converted **$50,000** in July **in-kind, 0% withholding**; paid est. tax (**~$11,000**) from cash
- Funded **$8,000 DAF** to improve itemized deductions (taxable income effect)
- Logged confirmations; set calendar for **Nov/Dec** review each year
- **Top-off $4,000** in November after CPA confirmed remaining headroom & IRMAA buffer

Outcome: predictable taxes **this** year, **no** IRMAA surprises **next** year, a **larger Roth** compounding at **0% tax**, and a slightly **smaller RMD** base — repeated annually, this becomes a quiet engine for lifetime tax savings.

Pro Tips, Scripts & Shortcuts (Pillar-2 specific)

Use these drop-in scripts, plus a few "gotchas" and follow-ups, to make execution fast and clean.

1) Email to CPA (conversion setup)

Subject options (pick one):

- Roth conversion: confirm max safe amount + basis check
- Bracket-fill conversion & IRMAA safe — numbers to confirm
- Quick review: 22%/24% headroom, Form 8606, and conversion amount

Body (copy/paste):
Hi [Name] — Please confirm my max safe Roth conversion for this year that keeps me in the [22%/24%] bracket and below the next IRMAA tier, with a ~$[2–5]k buffer. Also: do I have any IRA basis on file (Form 8606)? If yes, advise on isolating basis (roll pre-tax to 401(k) if allowed) before converting. Plan: 0% withholding, taxes paid from cash. Please reply with the exact dollar amount, timing guidance, and any state-tax considerations. Thanks!

Attach/Include:

- Your Pillar-1 worksheet (top-of-bracket, projected taxable income, headroom, IRMAA buffer)
- YTD income summary (W-2/1099s, dividends/gains to date)
- List of IRA/401(k) balances and custodians

Fast follow-up (if no reply in 3 days):
Friendly nudge on my Roth conversion numbers — hoping to schedule this for [date]. Can you confirm the amount that keeps me under the [22%/24%] bracket top and below IRMAA with a $[buffer] margin?

2) Email to plan administrator (basis isolation / roll-in)
Subject: Does the 401(k) accept pre-tax IRA roll-ins?
Body:
Hi — Does my 401(k) accept roll-ins of pre-tax IRA dollars? If so, what is the process, forms, and typical timeline? Goal: roll in pre-tax amounts only, then convert the remaining after-tax basis in my IRA to Roth. Please confirm any fees, trading blackout periods, and whether you track pre-/after-tax sources separately. Thanks!
If the plan says "no": ask your CPA about alternatives (e.g., different employer plan that does accept roll-ins; if you have self-employment income, a solo 401(k) may allow roll-ins — confirm with a provider).

3) Email for in-plan Roth conversion (IRR)
Subject: In-plan Roth conversion request
Body:
Hi — I'd like to complete an in-plan Roth conversion of $[amount]. Please confirm: • The steps and form to initiate an IRR • Whether I can convert specific holdings in-kind • Any plan-specific five-year rules or distribution restrictions • Processing timeline and confirmation details.

4) Custodian call / secure message (execute conversion)

Call script:
Please convert $[amount] from my Traditional IRA to my Roth IRA, in-kind, with 0% tax withholding. List the positions to move as: [fund/ETF/ticker/number of shares]. Process on [date]/at market close, and email me written confirmation showing the exact amount, date, and positions transferred.
Secure message (same content):
Roth conversion request — $[amount], in-kind, 0% withholding. Positions: [list]. Date: [mm/dd]. Please confirm in writing. Thanks!
Voicemail backup:
This is [Full Name], account ending [xxxx]. Please call back to confirm my Roth conversion request: $[amount], in-kind, 0% withholding, process on [date]. My number is [phone].

5) Two guardrails (expanded)

- **IRMAA guard:** Leave **$1k–$5k** below the next tier. If your fund pays a surprise year-end capital-gain distribution, that buffer saves you.
- **Bracket guard:** Leave **$2k–$5k** under your target bracket top. Don't "use every dollar" of headroom — estimates move.

When to override: Only with a clear reason (e.g., unique legacy goal, state-tax change, or one-time deduction that offsets the jump). Document the rationale with your CPA.

6) Year-end surprises to watch

- **Capital-gains distributions** in taxable mutual funds (often **December**); re-check headroom after they hit.
- **Unexpected 1099-DIV/INT** bumps; some funds pay more than last year.
- **Property sales / bonuses / RSU vests** late in the year.
- **RMD timing** (if applicable): you **must take RMD first**; it cannot be converted.

7) Tax payment strategy (so the Roth isn't "shrunk")

- Set conversion **withholding to 0%**; pay tax from **cash** or an **estimated payment**.
- To avoid underpayment penalties, you can:
  - Satisfy the **safe harbor** (e.g., 100%/110% of last year's tax), or
  - Temporarily **increase W-2 withholding** late in the year (treated as paid evenly all year).

8) After-action email to CPA (paper trail)

Subject: Roth conversion done — please note for 1099-R/5498/8606

Body:

Hi [Name] — I executed a Roth conversion of $[amount] on [date], in-kind, 0% withholding. Please note for year-end/tax prep (1099-R, 5498, and Form 8606 if basis applies). Current estimate is $[tax estimate] federal (+ state $[x] if applicable). Let me know if you recommend a supplemental estimate.

9) One-sheet log (keep this with your records)

Conversion Log — Part A

Date	Amount	In-kind?	Withholding	Positions moved
__ /___ /20___	$________	☐ Yes ☐ No	____%	__________

Conversion Log — Part B

Headroom used	IRMAA buffer left	Est. tax (fed/state)	Confirm #
$________	$________	$________ / $________	__________

Notes____

Save: custodian confirmation PDF, later **1099-R** (distribution), **5498** (Roth receipt), and **Form 8606** if basis.

10) Quick decision prompts (when unsure)

- **Income changed since Pillar 1?** Re-run headroom; if narrower, trim amount.
- **Close to IRMAA?** Trim to keep a **$1k–$5k buffer**.
- **Have basis?** Don't convert until you've decided whether to **isolate basis**.
- **Market down 10–15%?** If buffers remain, consider a **top-off** to shift rebound to Roth.
- **RMD year?** Take **RMD first**, then convert amounts **above** RMD.

These templates + guardrails turn Pillar-2 execution into a repeatable, low-stress routine: confirm numbers, isolate basis if needed, convert **in-kind** with **0% withholding**, document, and set your **Nov/Dec true-up**.

Tools & Printables You'll Use

1) Roth Conversion Readiness Quiz
Purpose: Fast go/no-go signal and sizing (none / partial / ladder).
How to use: Check **Yes/No** for each item, total points, follow next-step guidance.
Print fields:

- ☐ 22%–24% bracket headroom (with buffer)
- ☐ Below next IRMAA tier (with buffer)
- ☐ Cash on hand for taxes (no withholding)
- ☐ Bridge year / lower income
- ☐ RMD reduction / legacy goal
- ☐ Clean mechanics (in-kind, in-plan OK)
- ☐ Comfortable holding conversion long-term

  Score box: ____ / 7 → **Decision:** ☐ Wait/test ☐ Partial ☐ Multi-year ladder

2) Conversion Worksheet (one page)
Purpose: Turn Pillar 1 outputs into an exact conversion order you can execute.
Sections & fields to fill:
A) Targets

Field	Value
Filing status	☐ Single ☐ MFJ
Target bracket	____%
Top-of-bracket $	
Projected Taxable Income $	
Headroom $ (Top-of-bracket − Projected Taxable)	
IRMAA Tier (this year's thresholds)	
Buffer goal $	

B) Basis & accounts

Item	Selection	Notes
IRA basis on Form 8606?	☐ Yes ☐ No	Year last filed: ____
Plan allows pre-tax roll-in?	☐ Yes ☐ No ☐ N/A	–
Source account for conversion	☐ Trad IRA ☐ 401(k)/403(b) (IRR)	–
Convert in-kind?	☐ Yes ☐ No	If **Yes**, list tickers/positions: __________

C) Amount & buffers

Field	Amount
Headroom $	________
Less bracket buffer $ (2–5k)	________
Planned conversion $	________
IRMAA check after conversion → MAGI est. $	________
Still below tier?	☐ Yes

D) Taxes & timing

Item	Value
Estimated Federal tax (conversion × rate)	$ ________
+ State tax	$ ________
Withholding	0% (pay from cash) ☐ Confirmed
Execution window	____ / ____ / ____ → ____ / ____ / ____
Market-dip trigger	"If portfolio − __% from recent high, convert up to $ ________ (stay within buffers)."

E) Documentation

Document / Action	Status
Custodian confirmation saved	☐ PDF ☐ Date: ____
Expect 1099-R / 5498	☐ Noted
8606 to file (if basis)	☐ Noted

3) CPA & Custodian Scripts (copy-paste pack)
Included templates:

- **CPA setup email** (confirm max safe amount, basis/8606, state-tax notes)
- **Plan administrator email** (roll-in / in-plan Roth steps)
- **Custodian call / secure message** (in-kind, 0% withholding, written confirmation)
- **Year-end true-up email** (confirm remaining headroom & IRMAA buffer for a top-off)

Tip: Print the scripts or keep a Notes doc; fill blanks once, reuse every year.

4) Year-End True-Up Checklist
Purpose: Capture leftover "safe" headroom in Nov–Dec without tripping brackets or IRMAA.

Step-by-step:

1. Update **YTD income** (W-2/1099, dividends, realized gains).
2. Re-compute **Projected Taxable** and **Headroom** vs. target bracket.
3. Re-check **IRMAA** with MAGI + proposed top-off (keep $1k–$5k buffer).
4. Scan for **fund capital-gains distributions** in taxable accounts (often Dec).
5. If safe, **top-off conversion** $: ________ (in-kind, 0% withholding).
6. Save confirmation; note new **1099-R/5498** entries for tax prep.

5) Execution Log (mini table)

Purpose: One glance shows what you did, when, and what's left.
Date | Amount | In-kind? | Withholding | Positions moved | Headroom used | IRMAA buffer left | Est. tax (fed/state) | Confirm ID | Notes

6) IRMAA Quick Reference Card

Purpose: Prevent premium surprises (two-year lookback).
Fields:

Field	**Value**
Filing status	☐ Single ☐ MFJ
Current IRMAA tier cutoffs $	__________
My MAGI est. before conversion $	__________
Planned conversion $	__________
Total MAGI $	__________
Buffer left $	__________

7) Market-Dip Trigger Card

Field	**Value**
Purpose	**Pre-decide action in volatility.**
Text to print	**"If portfolio declines __% from recent high, convert up to $ ________ (stay under bracket/IRMAA buffers). Use in-kind; 0% withholding; confirm in writing."**

8) One-Page "Go Kit" (what to print and keep together)

Item	Status / Date
Readiness Quiz (scored)	☐ Completed
Conversion Worksheet (completed & signed)	☐ Completed
CPA setup email	Sent date: ___ / ___ / ___
Custodian request	Sent date: ___ / ___ / ___
Execution Log	☐ Updated
Year-End True-Up Checklist	Calendar dates added
IRMAA Card & Market-Dip Card	☐ Included

With these pages filled, Pillar 2 becomes a rinse-and-repeat process: confirm numbers, convert in-kind with 0% withholding, document, and top-off safely at year-end.

Action Step (what to complete now)

Objective: leave this module with a **specific, scheduled** conversion you can execute confidently—sized to your bracket plan, **IRMAA** buffer, and long-term goal of more **tax-free** income.

1) Fill the Readiness Quiz & Conversion Worksheet

- **Planned conversion amount:** Use **Headroom − $2k–$5k buffer** = $________
- **IRMAA check:** MAGI (AGI + tax-exempt interest) **+** conversion stays **below** next tier **by $1k–$5k**? ☐ Yes
- **Account & positions:** Choose source (Trad IRA / 401k) and list **in-kind** positions (tickers + share counts).
- **Tax payment source:** ☐ Cash (preferred) ☐ Estimated payment ☐ Temporary W-2 withholding bump
- **Execution window:/** to**/** (avoid holidays/mutual-fund distribution dates)

2) Send the CPA email (confirm numbers & basis)

Copy/paste:
Subject: Confirm my max safe Roth conversion + basis (Form 8606) Hi [Name] — Please confirm my max safe Roth conversion that keeps me in the [22%/24%] bracket and below the next IRMAA tier with a ~$[2–5]k buffer. Do I have IRA basis on file (Form 8606)? If yes, advise on isolating basis (roll pre-tax to 401(k) if allowed) before converting. Plan: in-kind conversion, 0% withholding, taxes paid from cash. Thanks!

Attach your worksheet (Top-of-Bracket, Projected Taxable, Headroom, IRMAA buffer).

3) Place the conversion order in your execution window

- **Custodian/plan instruction (phone or secure message):** "Convert **$[amount]** from my Traditional IRA to my Roth IRA **in-kind, 0% withholding**. Positions: [tickers/shares]. Process on [date]. Please send written confirmation (date, amount, positions)."
- Save the **confirmation PDF** to your tax folder.

4) Line up tax payments (so the Roth isn't shrunk)

- Estimate federal: **Conversion × marginal rate** = $________ (+ state $________).
- Pay from **cash** (or adjust **estimates / withholding** to meet safe-harbor rules).
- Note in calendar: "Enter 1099-R & 5498; file Form 8606 if basis."

5) Put the follow-ups on your calendar

- **Mid-Year Review (May/June):** refresh income; re-check headroom.
- **Year-End True-Up (Nov/Dec):** ask CPA for **remaining safe headroom** and **IRMAA** margin → consider a **top-off conversion** before **12/31**.
- **Market-Dip Trigger:** create an alert: "If portfolio −10%/−15% from recent high → convert up to remaining headroom (stay within buffers)."

6) Update your Execution Log

Date | Amount | In-kind? | Withholding | Positions moved | Headroom used | IRMAA buffer left | Est. tax | Confirm ID | Notes

Quick example (filled-in)

- **Headroom:** $35,000 | **Buffer:** $3,000 → **Planned conversion: $32,000**
- **IRMAA:** MAGI after conversion is **$2,400** under next tier → ✅
- **Positions (in-kind):** VTI 110 sh, BND 90 sh
- **Tax plan:** Est. fed ≈ $7,040; pay from cash (0% withholding)
- **Execution window:** Oct 15–Oct 20
- **Market-dip trigger:** −12% → convert extra up to **$5,000** if buffer remains
- **Year-end true-up:** Dec 10 appointment with CPA

Done when…

- ☐ Readiness Quiz scored; Conversion Worksheet completed
- ☐ CPA email sent; numbers/basis confirmed (or pending)
- ☐ Conversion scheduled/executed **in-kind** with **0% withholding**
- ☐ Confirmation saved; tax folder prepped for **1099-R / 5498 / 8606**
- ☐ Mid-year & Nov/Dec reminders + market-dip alert on calendar

Deliverable: a **specific, scheduled** conversion amount you can carry out confidently—sized to your **bracket**, safe on **IRMAA**, and building your **tax-free** income engine.

Pillar 2 — Executive Summary

Introduction & Key Points

- **What it is:** Convert pre-tax IRA/401(k) dollars to a **Roth** so future growth/withdrawals are **tax-free** and **no RMDs** apply.
- **Focus:** Convert within a **target bracket**, stay under **IRMAA** tiers, pay taxes from **cash**, and favor **in-kind** moves.
- **When it shines:** Bridge years, market dips, legacy goals. **Pass** in high-income/IRMAA-tight years.

The Rationale (why)

- **Tax arbitrage:** Trade a **known rate now** for **0% later** if today's marginal rate ≤ future/ heirs' rates.
- **Optionality:** Roth = flexible, tax-free buffer during volatility (reduces sequence risk).
- **Pressure relief:** Shrinks future **RMDs** and **IRMAA** exposure.
- **Legacy:** Heirs avoid big taxable spikes (10-year rule still applies, but **tax-free** for Roth).

Published

- **Status:** Content is blueprint-ready with worksheets, scripts, and checklists to deploy immediately.

Readiness Quiz (score yourself quickly)

- 7 yes/no items covering **bracket headroom**, **IRMAA buffer**, **cash for tax**, **bridge years**, **RMD/legacy goals**, **mechanics**, **time horizon**.
- **0–2:** wait/test • **3–5:** partial (bracket-fill) • **6–7:** multi-year ladder.

Key Mechanics (what trips people up)

- **Pro-rata rule & Form 8606** (consider **basis isolation** via 401(k) roll-in).
- **Five-year clocks:** owner clock (earnings), conversion clock (penalty <59½).
- **No recharacterization:** conversions are **final**.
- **RMD sequencing:** take **RMD first**, then convert extras.
- **State tax & withholding:** set **0% withholding**, pay tax from cash.
- **Plan nuances:** in-plan Roth conversions, roll-ins, fees, distribution rules.

Step-by-Step Implementation (10–15 minutes)

1. Import Pillar-1 **headroom & IRMAA buffer**.
2. Check **basis/8606**; isolate if helpful.
3. Choose account & **in-kind** positions.
4. Pick amount = headroom − **$2k–$5k buffer**.
5. Line up **cash** for tax.
6. Execute with custodian (in-kind, **0% withholding**).
7. **Document** (confirmation, 1099-R, 5498, 8606).
8. **Nov/Dec true-up** for safe top-off.

Real-World Examples (short & practical)

- **Kim (62):** Clean IRA, converts **$40k**; dip trigger for **$10k**.
- **Carlos (64): Isolates basis** via 401(k) roll-in; converts **$20k** basis, minimal tax.
- **Priya (67):** High-income year; **waits**, plans bigger conversion next year.
- **Dana (66): In-plan** Roth conversion **$25k** while contributing pre-tax.

Mini Case Story (narrative)

- **Ray (68) & Dana (66):** Headroom **$55k**; convert **$50k** in-kind, add **$8k DAF**, year-end **$4k** top-off.
- **Outcome:** smaller RMDs, no IRMAA jump, growing Roth for **0%** withdrawals.

Pro Tips, Scripts & Shortcuts (Pillar-2 specific)

- **Emails:** CPA (max safe amount + basis), plan admin (roll-ins), custodian (in-kind, 0% withholding), year-end true-up.
- **Guardrails:** keep **$2k–$5k** under bracket top and **$1k–$5k** under IRMAA tier; watch **December fund distributions**.
- **Tax strategy:** hit **safe harbor** or adjust withholding; never shrink the Roth with withholding if avoidable.

Tools & Printables You'll Use

- **Readiness Quiz, Conversion Worksheet, CPA/Plan/Custodian scripts, Year-End True-Up Checklist, Execution Log, IRMAA & Market-Dip cards.**

Action Step (what to complete now)

- Fill Quiz & Worksheet; set **planned conversion** (below headroom), pick **in-kind positions**, define **cash tax plan** and **execution window**.
- Send **CPA email**; schedule **Nov/Dec true-up** and **−10%/−15%** dip alert.
- **Deliverable:** a specific, scheduled conversion aligned with your **bracket plan**, **IRMAA buffer**, and **tax-free income** goal.

Pillar 3 — Timing Your Conversion for Maximum Savings

Introduction and Key Points

Converting is only half the game – **timing** decides how much you actually keep. This pillar shows you how to spread conversions across the **right years** and **right amounts** so you fill your target bracket (not more), avoid **IRMAA** cliffs, and capture the biggest **lifetime** tax savings. You'll turn guesswork into a simple, repeatable **multi-year ladder** with buffers and built-in rules for market dips.

What you'll do in this module

- Map the next **3–5 years** (bridge years, Social Security start, RMD age, known income events).
- Use **bracket filling** to size this year's conversion and set amounts for future years.
- Add safety margins for **IRMAA** and surprise income.
- Create a **market-dip trigger** so rebounds grow tax-free in Roth.
- Schedule **mid-year** and **Nov/Dec** reviews for a clean year-end top-off.

What to have handy

- Your Pillar 1 outputs: **Top-of-bracket**, **Projected taxable income**, **Headroom**, **IRMAA buffer**.
- Expected dates for **Social Security** and **RMDs**.
- Any known one-time events (property sale, large medical expenses, charitable plans).
- Current portfolio snapshot (to set a practical **dip trigger**).

Your outcome

By the end of Pillar 3, you'll have a **dated, dollar-specific 3–5 year conversion ladder** and a **this-year amount** sized to your bracket and IRMAA buffers – plus a one-line rule for when to **convert more** during market downturns.

Key Points

- **Use "Bracket Filling."**
    - Estimate your taxable income for the year.
    - Identify your *target* top tax bracket (e.g., 12%, 22%, 24%).

- Convert **only** the dollar amount that fills the remaining room in that bracket (not a dollar more).
- **Mind IRMAA (Medicare surcharges).**
  - Conversions increase MAGI used for IRMAA two years later.
  - If you're near a threshold, cap the conversion *below* that tier or split across 2–3 years. *(Check current-year thresholds before finalizing.)*

Coordinate with Social Security.

Before claiming benefits (or in low-income "bridge years" between retirement and RMD age), you often have **extra headroom** for larger conversions.

- After claiming, conversions can increase the taxation of Social Security—model both ways.
- **Capitalize on Low-Income or Market-Dip Windows.**
  - Years with one-time deductions, business losses, or a sabbatical = **bigger conversion room**.
  - Market pullbacks let you convert more shares at lower values, shifting future rebounds into the Roth.
- **Bunching & Offsets.**
  - Pair conversions with **charitable bunching** or Donor-Advised Fund contributions to offset added income.
  - Harvest capital **losses** (taxable accounts) in the same year to lower overall tax impact.
- **RMD Clock & Age Milestones.**
  - Start earlier to **shrink future RMDs** (and future IRMAA risk).
  - Once RMDs begin, you must take the RMD **first**; only amounts above that can be converted.
- **Multi-Year Ladder, Not One-Shot.**
  - A 3–7 year **conversion ladder** usually beats a single large conversion by smoothing taxes and avoiding threshold cliffs.

Why This Matters for Retirees

- **Minimizes Lifetime Taxes (not just this year).** Smart timing can save six figures over 20–30 years.
- **Controls Healthcare Costs.** Avoiding IRMAA jumps keeps Medicare premiums predictable.
- **Stabilizes Net Income.** Smoother, bracket-aware conversions reduce the chance of surprise tax bills and benefit phase-outs.
- **Protects Your Legacy.** Smaller pre-tax balances mean fewer forced withdrawals and more tax-free assets for heirs.

Action Step
Complete the **Tax Bracket Filler Planner** (5–10 minutes):

1. **Project This Year's Income**
   - Wages/consulting, pensions, interest/dividends, rental, estimated capital gains, planned deductions.
2. **Pick Your Target Bracket & Limits**
   - Write down the *top* dollar of your chosen bracket and the **current IRMAA threshold** for your filing status. *(Look up current figures.)*
3. **Calculate Your Headroom**
   - Target-Bracket Top − Projected Taxable Income = **Max Safe Conversion** (before hitting the next bracket).
   - If within ~$2–$5k of an **IRMAA tier**, reduce the conversion to stay safely below it.

4. **Set a Multi-Year Ladder**
   - Repeat steps 1–3 for the next 3–5 years (assume SSA start date, RMD age, and any one-time deductions).
   - Allocate larger conversions to **bridge years** (post-work, pre-SSA/RMD).
   - Note any planned **DAF/charitable** gifts or capital-loss harvesting to offset conversions.
5. **Market-Dip Trigger (Optional)**
   - Add a rule: "If portfolio declines ≥10–15% from recent high, execute an **extra** conversion up to remaining headroom."

When you're done, you'll have a clear **dollar amount to convert this year** and a **3–5 year conversion ladder** that maximizes savings while dodging bracket and IRMAA cliffs.

The Rationale (the "why" in plain English)

1) Taxes change over decades, not just this year
Your bracket, deductions, and benefits evolve as you stop working, start Social Security, hit RMD age, or face healthcare costs. If you only optimize for "this year," you can miss cheap opportunities that appear in **bridge years** (post-work, pre-SS/RMD).

- *Mini-map idea:* Mark the next 5–7 years with: last paycheck year, SS start, RMD start, known one-offs (property sale, big medical, charity plans).
- *Quick example:* In a year with no wages and no SS, your taxable income may be low enough to convert **$30k–$60k** and still stay in your target bracket—an opening that disappears once SS/RMDs begin.

2) Sequence-of-returns risk: use dips to your advantage
Markets don't rise in a straight line. Converting **more** in down years shifts the **rebound** into Roth, where growth is **tax-free**; converting **less** in overheated markets preserves room for a better entry later.

- *Rule of thumb:* Add a "dip trigger." Example: "If portfolio drops **10–15%**, convert up to remaining headroom (still under bracket and IRMAA buffers)."
- *Why it works:* You're not market-timing; you're **policy-timing**—using volatility to place future gains where they won't be taxed.

3) Threshold cliffs make tiny mistakes expensive
Tax and benefit rules have cliffs: cross them by **$1** and you can owe hundreds or thousands more (e.g., **IRMAA** surcharges, bracket jumps, credit/ deduction phase-outs). Good timing keeps **buffers**.

- *Practice:* Leave **$2k–$5k** below your target bracket top and **$1k–$5k** below the next IRMAA tier.
- *Example math:* If your headroom is **$35,000**, convert **$30k–$33k**, not the full **$35k**. That $2k–$5k cushion protects you from surprise dividends, capital-gain distributions, or last-minute income.

4) Compounding rewards earlier—but only within guardrails
Earlier conversions buy more **years of tax-free growth**. But converting so much that you spill into a higher bracket or over an IRMAA tier can erase the advantage. The win is **steady, bracket-aware, multi-year** execution.

- *Mini-math:* Convert **$40,000** at **22%** → tax **$8,800** (40,000 × 0.22 = 8,800). If that $40k doubles to **$80,000** in Roth, you withdraw **$80,000 tax-free** later. If left pre-tax and withdrawn at **24%**, tax would be **$19,200** (80,000 × 0.24). Directionally, paying **$8,800** now vs **$19,200** later keeps **$10,400** in your pocket (19,200 − 8,800 = 10,400).
- *Guardrails:* Earlier **yes**, but not at the cost of a higher bracket or an IRMAA jump. Use buffers every year.

Bottom line: Timing isn't about predicting markets or Congress. It's about **planning windows**, **filling brackets**, **avoiding cliffs**, and letting **time in Roth** do the heavy lifting—year after year.

Key Points (what to optimize)

1) Use "Bracket Filling"
Goal: convert **up to** the top of your target bracket—**not over**.

- **Step-by-step:**
    1. **Estimate Projected Taxable Income** for this year.

2. Look up the **Top-of-Bracket** dollar for your filing status (e.g., 22% or 24%).
3. **Headroom = Top-of-Bracket − Projected Taxable.**
4. Subtract a **$2k–$5k safety buffer** to protect against surprises.

- **Mini-example:** If Top-of-Bracket = $190,000 and Projected Taxable = $155,000 → Headroom = **$35,000** (190,000 − 155,000 = 35,000). With a $3,000 buffer, **convert $32,000**.
- **Pro tip:** Don't chase the last dollar of headroom; leave breathing room for year-end dividends or capital-gains distributions.

2) Mind IRMAA (Medicare) with the 2-year lookback

Why: This year's **MAGI** affects premiums **two years later**.

- **Rule of thumb:** Stay **$1k–$5k below** the next IRMAA tier.
- **Check:**
  - **MAGI = AGI + tax-exempt interest.**
  - Add your planned conversion and confirm you're still **under** the tier **by a buffer**.
- **Example:** If your IRMAA cutoff is $206,000, aim to cap total MAGI at **$201k–$205k**, not $205,999.

3) Coordinate with Social Security (SS)

- **Before claiming SS:** You often have **extra headroom** → consider **larger** conversions.
- **After claiming SS:** Conversions can increase how much of SS is taxed; **model both ways** (with and without the conversion).
- **Practical cue:** If you plan to start SS in two years, consider **front-loading conversions** now while room is wider.

4) Capitalize on low-income or market-dip windows

- **Low-income years:** Sabbatical, consulting gap, large deductions = **bigger conversions** at lower rates.
- **Market dips:** If portfolio declines **10–15%**, consider a **top-off conversion** (within buffers) so the **rebound compounds tax-free** in Roth.
- **Trigger line to print:** "If portfolio −__% from recent high → convert up to $____ (stay under bracket & IRMAA buffers)."

5) Use offsets to improve the trade

- **Charitable bunching / DAF:** Bundle several years of giving into **one** conversion year to boost itemized deductions.

- **Capital-loss harvesting:** In taxable accounts, realize losses to offset gains and up to **$3,000** of ordinary income.
- **Medical timing:** Large expenses above **7.5% of AGI** in one year can increase deductions—pair with conversions.
- **HSA contributions (if eligible):** Triple tax advantage; helpful in conversion years.
- **Note:** Offsets can reduce your **tax bill**, but some (like DAF) **do not reduce MAGI** and won't help with **IRMAA**—plan IRMAA separately.

6) RMD clock & age milestones

- **Before RMDs:** Best time to **shrink the future RMD base** with conversions.
- **Once RMDs begin:** You **must take the RMD first**; only amounts **above** that can be converted.
- **Age flags to calendar: 65** (Medicare), **SS start**, **RMD age**—your conversion room typically **shrinks** after each.

7) Plan a multi-year ladder (3–7 years)

- **Why: Smoother taxes** beat a one-time spike. Spread conversions to stay under brackets and IRMAA each year.
- **How:**
  - Map **bridge years** (bigger conversions).
  - Downshift in **SS/RMD** years (smaller conversions).
  - **Re-check annually**—income, markets, and thresholds move.
- **Template columns to use:**
  Year | Bridge year? | Target bracket | Planned conversion | Offsets (DAF/loss/medical) | IRMAA-safe? | Notes (SS/RMD)

Bottom line: Optimize **amounts and timing**—fill (don't spill) your bracket, stay **under IRMAA** with a built-in buffer, lean into **low-income/market-dip** years, and commit to a **multi-year ladder** that you true-up each November.

Step-by-Step Implementation (10–15 minutes)

Goal: build a **3–5 year conversion ladder** sized to your **target bracket** and **IRMAA** buffers, with a simple annual playbook you'll actually follow.

Minute 0–3 — Map your next 5 years
Create a 1-line-per-year timeline. You're looking for **windows** (cheap years) and **pinch points** (room shrinks).

Fill this quick grid:

Year	Working?	SS start?	RMD?	Big events (sale/medical/charity)
20__	Y/N	Y/N	Y/N	____________________
20__	Y/N	Y/N	Y/N	____________________
20__	Y/N	Y/N	Y/N	____________________
20__	Y/N	Y/N	Y/N	____________________
20__	Y/N	Y/N	Y/N	____________________

Notes: ______________________________________

Interpretation:

- **Bridge years** (post-work, pre-SS/RMD) = bigger conversions.
- **SS/RMD years** = smaller conversions.
- One-offs (property sale, big deductible medical expense, planned DAF gift) = **opportunities** to convert **more** that year.

Minute 4–6 — For this year, compute the number

Pull your Pillar-1 figures and do the math once (don't overthink it).

Write these down:

- **Top-of-bracket ($):** ________
- **Projected taxable ($):** ________
- **Headroom = Top − Taxable =** $ ________
- **Subtract buffer ($2k–$5k) → Planned conversion =** $ ________

IRMAA check:

- **MAGI est. = AGI + tax-exempt interest + planned conversion**
- Am I **$1k–$5k below** the next IRMAA tier after adding the conversion? ☐ **Yes** ☐ No → **Trim amount**

Micro-example:

Top-of-bracket $190,000; Projected taxable $155,000 → Headroom $35,000.
Buffer $3,000 → **Planned conversion $32,000**.
IRMAA tier $206,000; MAGI after conversion $203,400 → **Buffer $2,600 (OK).**

Minute 7–9 — Rough-plan the next 2–4 years

You're not predicting; you're **pre-allocating** space.

Rules of thumb:

- **SS start year** and **RMD years** → plan **smaller** conversions.
- **Bridge years** → plan **larger** conversions.
- Pencil in **offsets** where they fit (DAF bunching in Year 1, potential capital-loss harvesting in a down year, large medical expenses).

Sketch table:

Year	Bridge?	Target bracket	Planned conv.	IRMAA-safe?	Offsets (DAF / loss / medical / HSA)
20__	Yes/No	22% / 24%	$______	☐ Yes	____________________
20__	Yes/No	22% / 24%	$______	☐ Yes	____________________
20__	Yes/No	22% / 24%	$______	☐ Yes	____________________
20__	Yes/No	22% / 24%	$______	☐ Yes	____________________

Notes: ____

Minute 10–12 — Add a market-dip trigger

Pre-decide how you'll act in volatility so you're **consistent**.

Print this on your worksheet:

"If my portfolio declines __% from the recent high, I will convert **up to $** ________ (remaining headroom), **in-kind**, with **0% withholding**, ensuring I stay below my **bracket** and **IRMAA** buffers."

Tips:

- Common triggers: **−10%** or **−15%**.
- Confirm headroom & IRMAA again **before** the top-off.

Minute 13–15 — Calendar touchpoints (make it automatic)

Set three repeating reminders:

1. **Mid-Year Check (May/June)**
   - Update YTD income and **re-estimate headroom**.
   - Adjust the planned amount if income surprised you.
2. **Nov/Dec True-Up (year-end)**
   - Ask CPA: "How much **safe headroom** remains under my target bracket and below IRMAA?"

- If clear, execute a **small top-off conversion** before **12/31**.
- Watch for **capital-gains distributions** in taxable funds (often December) before topping off.

3. **"Room Shrinks" Flags**
    - **SS claim date** and **RMD start** get calendar alerts 90 days prior to remind you that conversion room will likely **narrow**.

Example: 3-Year Ladder (filled-in sample)
(Illustrative numbers; use your own tables.)

Year	Bridge?	Target Bracket	Planned Conv.	IRMAA-safe?	Offsets	Notes
2025	Yes	22%	$48,000	Yes ($2k buf)	DAF $7,500	Market-dip trigger −12% up to +$6k
2026	Yes	22%	$45,000	Yes ($3k buf)	Loss harvesting if dip	SS starts 2027 → room shrinks
2027	No (SS)	22%	$28,000	Yes ($2k buf)	—	Recheck brackets in Nov

Recheck brackets in Nov

Done when you have:

- This year's **planned conversion** (with buffers),
- A **2–4 year** outline that scales up/down around SS/RMD years,
- A printed **dip trigger**, and
- **Mid-year** + **Nov/Dec** reminders on your calendar.

Real-World Examples (quick + practical)

Numbers are illustrative so you can see the mechanics. Always plug in your actual bracket tops, IRMAA tiers, and current-year income.

1) Pre-SS window = bigger moves — *Jordan (64) & Mei (63)*

- **Snapshot:** Retired; no Social Security yet; moderate dividends only.
- **Lane (from Pillar 1):** Headroom in **22%** ≈ **$60,000**; IRMAA buffer ≈ **$3,000**.
- **Plan:** Convert **$55,000/yr for 3 years**, leaving a **$5,000** safety buffer. Add **$10,000** DAF in Year 1 to boost itemized deductions (DAF doesn't lower MAGI/IRMAA; they already confirmed IRMAA safety).
- **Tax ballpark:** $55,000 × 22% = **$12,100** federal per year (plus state). Over 3 years ≈ **$36,300**.

- **Why now:** These are **bridge years**—no wages, no SS, no RMDs—so the bracket room is widest.
- **Directional impact:** Move **$165,000** pre-tax → Roth in 3 years. If first-year RMD factor is ~4%, that's about **$6,600/yr** less forced income at RMD start (0.04 × 165,000 = **6,600**), and growing Roth compounding at **0%** tax.

2) Post-SS = smaller, steady moves — *Alice (70)*

- **Snapshot:** Claimed Social Security at 68; RMD begins at 73.
- **Constraint:** SS adds to MAGI; IRMAA buffer is tighter.
- **Plan:** Convert **$20,000–$25,000/yr for 3 years**, each time leaving **$2k–$3k** under both bracket top and IRMAA tier.
- **Tax ballpark:**
    - $20,000 × 22% = **$4,400**
    - $25,000 × 22% = **$5,500**
- **Directional impact:** Reduce pre-tax by **$60k–$75k** before RMD age → first RMD drops by ~**$2,400–$3,000/yr** (0.04 × $60k–$75k) while keeping premiums steady.

3) RMD already started — *Ron (75)*

- **Snapshot:** RMD this year = **$19,200**; wants to keep building Roth without IRMAA surprises.
- **Sequence rule: Take the $19,200 RMD first** (taxable). The RMD **cannot** be converted.
- **Plan:** After distributing the RMD, convert **$15,000** more (staying under bracket and IRMAA buffers).
- **Enhancement (charitable):** If Ron gives to charity, he can do part of the RMD as a **QCD** (e.g., **$6,000** direct from IRA to charity). The QCD **satisfies** that portion of the RMD **without increasing MAGI**, helping IRMAA—then he still converts the separate **$15,000**.
- **Tax ballpark on the conversion:** $15,000 × 22% = **$3,300** (plus state).
- **Directional impact:** Keeps IRMAA stable, trims future pre-tax balance, and uses QCD to prevent the RMD from bloating MAGI.

4) Market-dip top-off — *Kim (62)*

- **Snapshot:** Planned conversion **$32,000** based on headroom and buffers.
- **Event:** Portfolio falls **12%** mid-year.
- **Action:** CPA rechecks headroom; **$6,000** remains safely under bracket/IRMAA. Kim executes a **$6,000 top-off** (in-kind, 0% withholding).
- **Totals & tax:**
    - Original: $32,000 × 22% = **$7,040**

   - Top-off: $6,000 × 22% = **$1,320**
   - **Year total tax ≈ $8,360** (plus state).
- **Why this works:** The rebound from the dip now compounds **inside Roth** tax-free, and she still preserves buffers.

Guardrails these examples share

- Leave **$2k–$5k** below your target bracket top and **$1k–$5k** below the next **IRMAA** tier.
- Prefer **in-kind** conversions with **0% withholding** (pay tax from cash).
- Add **Nov/Dec true-up** to capture remaining safe headroom—but watch for **December mutual-fund distributions** in taxable accounts before topping off.

Mini Case Story — "Ladder that avoids the cliffs"

Nora (64) & Sam (65)

- **Status:** Retired. Plan to start Social Security at **67/66**. **RMDs** begin at **73**.
- **From Pillar 1:** Headroom this year in the **22%** bracket = **$52,000**; **IRMAA buffer ≈ $3,000**.
- **Objective:** Move steady chunks to Roth **without** crossing tax or IRMAA thresholds; keep withdrawals flexible and tax-free later.

Year 1 (ages 64/65) — Use the wide "bridge-year" space

- **Conversion: $48,000** (leaves a **$4,000** safety margin under the bracket top and IRMAA tier).
- **Method: In-kind**, 0% withholding; taxes paid from cash.
- **Estimated federal tax:** $48,000 × 22% = **$10,560**. *(Check: 48 × .22 = 10.56 → add three zeros.)*
- **Charitable bunching:** Fund **$7,500** to a **DAF** to improve itemized deductions. *(Helpful for the tax bill; note DAF **does not** reduce MAGI, so it doesn't help IRMAA.)*
- **Result:** Big first step with buffers intact.

Year 2 — Engage the dip, keep buffers

- **Market event:** Portfolio draws down ~**10%** mid-year.
- **Headroom check:** Still ample.
- **Conversion: $50,000** planned **+ $5,000** dip **top-off** once CPA confirms room → **$55,000** total.
- **Method:** In-kind, 0% withholding.
- **Estimated federal tax:** $55,000 × 22% = **$12,100**. *(55 × .22 = 12.1 → add three zeros.)*

- **Planning note:** Sam will start **Social Security next year**, so they note "**room shrinks**" in Year 3.

Year 3 — After Social Security starts: stay under the cliffs

- **Constraint:** SS now increases MAGI; IRMAA buffer tighter.
- **Conversion: $28,000** (CPA confirms this keeps them ~**$2,000 under** the next IRMAA tier and below bracket top).
- **Method:** In-kind, 0% withholding.
- **Estimated federal tax:** $28,000 × 22% = **$6,160**.
- **Result:** Smaller, steady conversion that preserves premiums and avoids bracket creep.

Three-year recap (directional)

- **Total converted to Roth:** $48,000 + $55,000 + $28,000 = **$131,000**.
- **Total est. federal tax paid:** $10,560 + $12,100 + $6,160 = **$28,820**.
- **RMD base trimmed:** About **4%** of the amount moved will **not** be forced out as taxable income in the first RMD year.
    - **Illustration:** 0.04 × $131,000 = **$5,240** less **forced** income in Year 1 of RMDs.
    - *Digit check:* 131,000 × 4% = (131,000 × 4) / 100 = 524,000 / 100 = **5,240**.

Why this ladder works

- **Fills, doesn't spill:** They convert **up to** the 22% bracket with a **$2k–$5k buffer** each year.
- **IRMAA-safe:** MAGI stays **below** the next tier (buffer kept), so premiums don't jump two years later.
- **Dip rule adds value:** The **−10%** trigger in Year 2 shifts more future rebound into **tax-free Roth** without breaking buffers.
- **DAF timing smart:** Bunching gifts into a conversion year **improves itemizing** and lowers the tax bill (again, not MAGI).
- **Paper trail clean:** In-kind moves, 0% withholding, custodian confirmations saved; expect **1099-R**, **5498**, and file **Form 8606** as needed.

Their one-page playbook (what they actually did)

- **Year 1:** Convert **$48k** in-kind; DAF **$7.5k**; tax ≈ **$10,560**.
- **Year 2:** Convert **$50k** + **$5k** dip top-off; tax ≈ **$12,100**; note SS starts **next** year.
- **Year 3:** Convert **$28k** after SS; tax ≈ **$6,160**; buffers preserved.
- **Every November:** CPA confirms remaining **safe headroom** for a possible **top-off** before 12/31.

- **Outcome:** Smaller future **RMDs**, **no IRMAA surprises**, and a steadily growing **Roth** they can tap at **0%** during market volatility.

Pro Tips, Scripts & Shortcuts (timing-specific)

Use these copy-paste templates and micro-checklists to keep your **multi-year timing** tight and IRMAA-safe.

1) Email to CPA — multi-year timing check

Subject options (pick one):

- Multi-year Roth timing plan — bracket-fill & IRMAA safe
- Validate 3–5 yr conversion ladder (headroom + buffers)
- Quick review: 22%/24% headroom, SS/RMD years, and offsets

Body (copy/paste):

Hi [Name] — Please validate my 3–5 year Roth conversion ladder and confirm each year stays in the **[22%/24%]** bracket and **below the next IRMAA tier** with a ~**$[2–5]k** buffer.

This Year (20__)

Item	Amount
Top-of-bracket	$____
Projected taxable income	$____
Headroom (Top − Projected)	$____
Proposed conversion	**$____**
Bracket buffer (target $2–5k)	$[2–5]k
IRMAA buffer after conversion	**$____**

Next 2–4 Years (Plan)

Year	Target Bracket	Planned Conversion	IRMAA-Safe Buffer ($)	Offsets to Consider (DAF / Loss / Medical / HSA)
20__	[22%/24%]	$____	$____	____________________
20__	[22%/24%]	$____	$____	____________________
20__	[22%/24%]	$____	$____	____________________
20__	[22%/24%]	$____	$____	____________________

Milestones

Social Security start	RMD start
20__	20__

Please confirm amounts for each year and flag opportunities to improve timing (DAF bunching, loss harvesting, medical timing, HSA), plus any state-tax considerations. Thanks!

Attach/include:

- Pillar-1 worksheet (top-of-bracket, projected taxable, headroom, IRMAA tier).
- Simple 3–5 year ladder table.
- YTD income snapshot (W-2/1099s, dividends/gains so far).

Fast follow-up (if no reply in 3 business days):
Friendly nudge on my Roth timing plan — hoping to schedule this year's conversion for [date]. Can you confirm the bracket- and IRMAA-safe amount and the next 2–4 year targets?

What a great CPA reply includes (ask for this explicitly):

- Exact **conversion dollar** for each year.
- Your **MAGI/IRMAA** estimate with buffer marked.
- Notes on **offsets** to deploy and **months** to consider them.
- A reminder about **state tax** and **safe-harbor**/withholding tweaks.

2) Year-end true-up (Nov/Dec)
Subject: Year-end Roth top-off — headroom & IRMAA check
Body (copy/paste):
Quick update request: please confirm my remaining safe headroom in the [22%/24%] bracket and below IRMAA. If clear, I'd like to top off by $[amount] before 12/31 (in-kind, 0% withholding). Please also check for any December fund capital-gains distributions in my taxable accounts that could affect headroom.

Mini checklist before you top-off:

- ☐ Update YTD income (dividends, cap gains realized, consulting).
- ☐ Ask about **mutual-fund distributions** (often mid/late December).
- ☐ Reconfirm **IRMAA** buffer ($1k–$5k).
- ☐ Execute **in-kind, 0% withholding**, save confirmation.

3) Market-dip trigger note (to self or advisor)
Sticky-note version (print this):
If portfolio −[10–15]% from recent high: 1) Check remaining headroom & IRMAA buffer with CPA/worksheet. 2) Convert up to $[amount] (in-kind, 0% withholding). 3) Save confirmation; log date/amount/positions.

Text you can send your advisor on a dip day:
Markets off ~[X]%. Can you confirm my remaining bracket headroom and IRMAA margin today? If safe, please convert up to $[amount], in-kind, 0% withholding, and send written confirmation.

4) One-pager you can hand your CPA (makes reviews faster)

Year	Status (Bridge/SS/RMD)	Target Bracket	Planned Conversion	IRMAA Buffer	Offsets (DAF/Loss/Medical/HSA)
20__	Bridge	22%	$________	$________	________________________________
20__	Bridge	22%	$________	$________	________________________________
20__	SS starts	22%	$________	$________	________________________________
20__	RMD begins	22%	$________	$________	________________________________

Notes: ____

5) Timing guardrails (print at the top of your ladder)

- **Bracket buffer:** Keep **$2k–$5k** under target bracket top.
- **IRMAA buffer:** Keep **$1k–$5k** under the next tier (two-year lookback).
- **SS/RMD years:** Expect **less** room; pre-plan smaller conversions.
- **December watch:** Check **fund distributions** before topping off.
- **Paper trail:** In-kind + **0% withholding**; save custodian **confirmation**, expect **1099-R / 5498**, file **8606** as needed.

6) Example (filled-in snippets you can mirror)

CPA email line items (this year):

- Top-of-bracket: **$190,000** | Projected taxable: **$155,000** → Headroom **$35,000**
- Proposed conversion: **$32,000** (leaving **$3,000** buffer)
- IRMAA tier: **$206,000** | MAGI after conversion: **$203,400** → Buffer **$2,600**

Dip trigger card:

- Trigger at **−12%**; top-off **up to $6,000** if headroom remains and IRMAA buffer **≥ $2,000.**

These small systems make your timing **automatic**: annual plan → mid-year check → dip trigger → year-end true-up, all while staying below **tax** and **IRMAA** cliffs.

Tools

& Printables You'll Use

1) Tax Bracket Filler Planner (per-year sheet)

Field	Value
Purpose	Size this year's conversion precisely and leave buffers.
How to use	Fill once in spring; update in Nov/Dec.

Blank template

Item	Entry
Year	_______
Filing Status	☐ Single ☐ MFJ
Top-of-Bracket ($)	__________
Projected Taxable Income ($)	__________
Headroom = Top − Taxable ($)	__________
Safety Buffer ($2k–$5k)	__________
Planned Conversion ($)	__________
IRMAA Tier Cutoff ($)	__________
MAGI Before Conversion ($)	__________
+ Planned Conversion ($)	__________
MAGI After Conversion ($)	__________
IRMAA Buffer Remaining ($)	__________
Status	☐ OK ☐ Trim amount
Notes (dividends, fund distributions, state tax)	________________________

One-line example

Top 22%	Proj. Taxable	Headroom	Buffer	Planned	IRMAA cutoff	MAGI after	IRMAA buffer	Status
190,000	155,000	35,000	3,000	32,000	206,000	203,400	2,600	OK

2) 3–5 Year Ladder Table

Year	Bridge year?	Target bracket	Planned conversion	Offsets (DAF / loss / medical / HSA)	IRMAA-safe?	Notes (SS/RMD)
20__	☐ Yes ☐ No	22% / 24%	$______	____________	☐ Yes ☐ No	______
20__	☐ Yes ☐ No	22% / 24%	$______	____________	☐ Yes ☐ No	______
20__	☐ Yes ☐ No	22% / 24%	$______	____________	☐ Yes ☐ No	______
20__	☐ Yes ☐ No	22% / 24%	$______	____________	☐ Yes ☐ No	______
20__	☐ Yes ☐ No	22% / 24%	$______	____________	☐ Yes ☐ No	______

Mini example

Year	Bridge year?	Target bracket	Planned conversion	Offsets	IRMAA-safe?	Notes
2025	Yes	22%	$48,000	DAF $7,500	Yes	Dip trigger −12% up to +$6k
2026	Yes	22%	$45,000	Loss harvest if dip	Yes	SS starts 2027 — room shrinks
2027	No (SS)	22%	$28,000	—	Yes	After SS; keep IRMAA buffer ≥ $2k

3) IRMAA Quick-Ref Card
Purpose: prevent premium surprises (2-year lookback). Keep this on top of your planner.
Blank

Field	Value
Purpose	Prevent premium surprises (2-year lookback). Keep this on top of your planner.
Filing Status	☐ Single ☐ MFJ
Next IRMAA Tier Cutoff ($)	__________
My MAGI Before Conversion ($)	__________
+ Planned Conversion ($)	__________
MAGI After Conversion ($)	__________
Target Buffer ($1k–$5k)	__________
Result	☐ OK (buffer kept) ☐ Too tight — trim conversion by $________

4) Market-Dip Trigger Card
Purpose: pre-decide actions in volatility so you're consistent.
Print this
If portfolio declines −__% from recent high: 1) Recheck bracket headroom & IRMAA buffer. 2) Convert up to $________ (in-kind, 0% withholding). 3) Save confirmation; log date/amount/positions. Guardrails: keep $2k–$5k under bracket top AND $1k–$5k under IRMAA tier.
Example: "If −12%, convert up to $6,000 (still under buffers)."

5) Calendar Template (set these as recurring)
Purpose: make timing automatic.
Events to add

- **Mid-Year Check (May/June):** Update YTD income, recompute headroom; adjust plan.
- **Year-End True-Up (Nov/Dec):** Ask CPA for remaining safe headroom & IRMAA margin; top-off if clear; check for **mutual-fund capital-gains distributions** before converting.
- **SS Claim Date (Reminder −90/−30 days):** note "room shrinks."

- **RMD Start (Reminder −90/−30 days):** take RMD **first**; only amounts above can be converted.
- **Market-Dip Watch:** set alerts at **−10%** and **−15%** from recent high.

6) One-Page Execution Log (keep with tax docs)
Purpose: clean paper trail for you and your CPA.
Date | Amount | In-kind? | Withholding | Positions moved | Headroom used | IRMAA buffer left | Est. tax (fed/state) | Confirm ID | Notes

7) Quick How-To (turn these into a spreadsheet)

- Create one **tab** per tool above.
- Freeze header rows; add data validation (e.g., "Yes/No") and conditional formatting to turn cells **red** if MAGI exceeds an IRMAA tier or conversion exceeds headroom minus buffer.
- Add a **Summary tab** that pulls:
  - This year's **Planned Conversion**, **MAGI after**, **IRMAA buffer**, and **True-Up capacity**.

With these pages filled, your timing system runs itself: plan once, check mid-year, top-off at year-end, and act automatically on market dips—always inside your bracket and IRMAA buffers.

Action Step (what to complete now)

Objective: walk away with a **dated, dollar-specific multi-year conversion ladder** you can execute confidently—sized to your bracket plan and **IRMAA** buffers.
1) Fill the Tax Bracket Filler Planner (this year + next 2–4 years)

- **This year:**

Top-of-bracket $	**Projected Taxable $**	**Headroom $ (Top − Projected)**
________	________	________
Safety buffer ($2k–$5k)	**Planned conversion (Headroom minus Buffer)**	**IRMAA check|MAGI $1k–$5k below next tier?** ☐ Yes ☐ No → Trim
________	________	_______

- **Future years (rough):** repeat those lines with your best estimates.

Tip: If your numbers are estimates, leave the **bigger buffer** (closer to $5k) to avoid bracket/IRMAA creep.

2) Mark bridge years vs SS/RMD years

- **Bridge years (post-work, pre-SS/RMD):** mark **larger conversions**.
- **SS or RMD years:** mark **smaller conversions** (room usually shrinks).
- Add notes where you expect **offsets** (DAF bunching, loss harvesting, large medical, HSA).

Mini table (fill now):

Year	Bridge?	Target Bracket	Planned Conversion	IRMAA-safe?	Offsets
20__	Yes/No	22% / 24%	$________	☐ Yes	________
20__	Yes/No	22% / 24%	$________	☐ Yes	________
20__	Yes/No	22% / 24%	$________	☐ Yes	________

Notes: ____

3) Add a market-dip trigger & schedule your reviews

- **Dip trigger (print this on your worksheet):**

"If portfolio declines __% from recent high, convert **up to $________** (remaining headroom), **in-kind, 0% withholding**, staying under **bracket** and **IRMAA** buffers."

- **Calendar (set recurring):**
    - **Mid-Year Check (May/June):** update YTD income → re-estimate headroom.
    - **Year-End True-Up (Nov/Dec):** ask CPA for **remaining safe headroom**; watch for **December fund distributions**; top-off if clear.
    - **Room-shrinks flags: SS claim date** and **RMD start** (90-day reminders).

4) Email your multi-year plan to your CPA (confirm amounts & IRMAA margins)

Subject: Multi-year Roth timing plan — bracket-fill & IRMAA safe

Hi [Name] — Please validate my 3–5 year Roth conversion ladder.

This Year (20__)

Top-of-bracket $	Projected taxable $	Headroom $ (Top − Projected)	Buffer ($2k–$5k)	Proposed conversion $	Next IRMAA tier $	MAGI after conversion $	IRMAA safety margin $	Safe conversion?
________	________	________	________	________	________	________	________	☐ Yes ☐ No

Notes (in-kind, 0% withholding, taxes from cash):

____

Key Dates

SS start (year)	RMD start (year)
20__	20__

Next 2–4 Years (Confirm bracket + IRMAA "safe amounts" and note opportunities)

Year	SS starts?	RMD starts?	Top-of-bracket $	Projected taxable $	Headroom $	Buffer $	Planned conversion $	Next IRMAA tier $	MAGI after conversion $	IRMAA margin $	Safe amount confirmed?	Opportunities (DAF bunching, loss harvesting, medical timing, HSA)
20__	☐	☐									☐ Yes ☐ No	
20__	☐	☐									☐ Yes ☐ No	
20__	☐	☐									☐ Yes ☐ No	
20__	☐	☐										

Please confirm the safe amounts for each year (bracket + IRMAA), and note any opportunities to use DAF bunching, loss harvesting, medical timing, or HSA. Plan is in-kind, 0% withholding, taxes paid from cash. Thanks!

Attach your **Planner** and **Ladder table**.

Quick example (illustrative)

- **This year:** Headroom **$35,000**; buffer **$3,000** → **Planned conversion $32,000**; IRMAA buffer after: **$2,600** → ✅
- **Next year (pre-SS):** plan **$30,000–$35,000** (leave buffer; consider DAF)
- **SS year:** plan **$22,000–$28,000** (room shrinks)

"Done" checklist

- ☐ This year's **Planned conversion** set (Headroom − Buffer)
- ☐ Next **2–4 years** penciled with larger amounts in **bridge years** and smaller in **SS/RMD** years
- ☐ **Market-dip trigger** written on the worksheet
- ☐ **Mid-year** & **Nov/Dec** reminders and **SS/RMD** flags on calendar
- ☐ **CPA email** sent with attachments

Deliverable: a **dated, dollar-specific multi-year conversion ladder** that maximizes lifetime savings while staying **under** tax brackets and **IRMAA** cliffs.

Pillar 3 — Executive Summary

Introduction & Key Points

- **Goal:** Time conversions across the right **years** and **amounts** to maximize lifetime savings.
- **Focus:** Fill (don't spill) your **target bracket**, keep an **IRMAA buffer**, use **bridge years** and **market dips**, and adjust annually.

The Rationale (why it matters)

- **Multi-year game:** Income/benefits change (retirement → SS → RMDs). Harvest low brackets when they appear.
- **Volatility edge:** Convert more on **dips** so rebounds grow **tax-free** in Roth.
- **Avoid cliffs:** $1 over a bracket/IRMAA tier can be costly—use small **buffers**.
- **Compounding:** Earlier conversions help, but not at the cost of crossing thresholds.

Key Points (what to optimize)

- **Bracket filling:** Compute **headroom** and leave a **$2k–$5k** safety gap.
- **IRMAA:** Two-year lookback; keep **$1k–$5k** below the next tier.
- **Social Security:** Bigger room **before** SS; smaller after—model both.
- **Windows:** Convert more in **low-income** years and on **10–15% market dips**.

- **Offsets:** DAF bunching, loss harvesting, medical timing, HSA (where eligible).
- **RMD sequencing:** Best before RMDs; once they start, take RMD **first**.
- **Multi-year ladder:** 3–7 years beats a one-time spike; re-check yearly.

Step-by-Step (10–15 minutes)

1. **Map 5 years:** work/SS/RMD/big events.
2. **This year's number:** headroom − buffer; confirm **IRMAA**.
3. **Next 2–4 years:** pencil larger **bridge-year** amounts; smaller SS/RMD years; note offsets.
4. **Dip trigger:** "If −%, **convert up to $** within buffers."
5. **Calendar:** mid-year check + Nov/Dec true-up; flag SS/RMD dates.

Real-World Examples

- **Pre-SS:** Jordan & Mei convert **$55k/yr × 3** with a DAF; use wide room now.
- **Post-SS:** Alice converts **$20–25k/yr** to trim RMDs without IRMAA creep.
- **RMD started:** Ron takes **RMD first**, then converts **$15k**; QCD can lower MAGI.
- **Market dip:** Kim adds a **$6k top-off** after a 12% drop—rebound grows in Roth.

Mini Case Story — "Ladder that avoids the cliffs"

- **Nora (64) & Sam (65):** $52k headroom, $3k IRMAA buffer.
  - Y1: **$48k + $7.5k DAF**
  - Y2: **$50k + $5k dip top-off**
  - Y3 (after SS): **$28k**
- **Outcome:** smaller future **RMDs**, no IRMAA surprises, bigger **tax-free** cushion.

Pro Tips, Scripts & Shortcuts

- **CPA email:** validate **3–5 year ladder**, confirm **bracket/IRMAA-safe** amounts, identify offsets.
- **Year-end note:** confirm remaining headroom; **top-off** if safe.
- **Dip day text:** "Markets −%. **Confirm headroom/IRMAA; convert up to $** in-kind, 0% withholding."

Tools & Printables

- **Tax Bracket Filler Planner, 3–5 Year Ladder Table, IRMAA Quick-Ref Card, Market-Dip Trigger Card, Calendar Template, Execution Log.**

Action Step (deliverable)

- Complete the **Planner** and **Ladder**, add **dip trigger** + calendar reviews, and email the plan to your **CPA** for confirmation.
- **Deliverable:** a **dated, dollar-specific multi-year conversion ladder** that stays under brackets and IRMAA cliffs while maximizing tax-free growth.

Pillar 4 — Avoiding the RMD Tax Trap

Introduction and Key Points

Required Minimum Distributions (RMDs) are the moment the tax code stops being optional. They're **forced withdrawals** from pre-tax accounts—taxable whether you need the cash or not—and they can quietly push you into **higher brackets**, trigger **Medicare IRMAA** surcharges, increase the taxation of **Social Security**, and even bump you into **capital-gains** or **NIIT** (3.8% Medicare surtax) thresholds. This pillar shows you how to **defuse** that tax pressure before and after RMDs begin.

What we'll solve in this module

- **Shrink the problem early:** How to use pre-RMD years to right-size pre-tax balances (via planned Roth conversions and smart withdrawals).
- **RMD mechanics without mistakes:** Which accounts aggregate (and which don't), sequencing rules (why you must **take the RMD first** before converting), and clean withholding so you avoid penalties.
- **Charitable relief valves:** How **Qualified Charitable Distributions (QCDs)** can satisfy part/all of your IRA RMD **without increasing MAGI** (and why QCDs can't go to a DAF).
- **Guardrail planning:** Keeping **buffers** below bracket tops, **IRMAA tiers**, and other cliffs—so one extra dollar doesn't cost hundreds more.
- **Cash-flow design:** Turning a mandatory withdrawal into a predictable, tax-aware paycheck (monthly/quarterly cadence that matches your spending).

What to have handy

- Your **account list** by type (Traditional IRA/401(k)/403(b), Roth, taxable) and rough balances.
- Your **Pillar 1–3 outputs**: target bracket, IRMAA buffer, and any planned conversions.
- Your **Social Security** start date and the year RMDs begin (for your situation).
- This year's **tax projection** and withholding/estimated-tax status.

Your outcome

By the end of Pillar 4 you'll have a simple, written **RMD game plan**: a pre-RMD "shrink strategy," an **RMD-year checklist** (what to take, when, and from where), a **QCD play** if you give to charity, and a **cash-flow calendar** that keeps you under tax and IRMAA cliffs—turning a tax trap into a managed, predictable expense.

Key Points

- **What RMDs Are:**
  - Once you hit age **73** (or 75 if born in 1960 or later), the IRS requires annual withdrawals from pre-tax retirement accounts (Traditional IRAs, 401(k)s, 403(b)s, etc.).
  - The percentage you must withdraw **increases every year** as you age.
- **Why They're a Problem:**
  - They add taxable income whether you need the money or not.
  - Can push you into a higher tax bracket.
  - May trigger **IRMAA surcharges** on Medicare premiums.
  - Can cause more of your Social Security benefits to be taxed.
- **How to Shrink or Eliminate Them:**
  - **Roth Conversions Before RMD Age** — Moving pre-tax funds into a Roth IRA now reduces your future RMD base. Roth IRAs have *no* lifetime RMDs.
  - **Qualified Charitable Distributions (QCDs)** — After age 70½, you can donate directly from your IRA to charity, satisfying RMD requirements *without* adding taxable income.
  - **Strategic Withdrawals in Lower Tax Years** — Taking some distributions in low-income years before RMD age can reduce future RMD size.
  - **Use Employer Plans to Delay RMDs** — If still working past 73 and own less than 5% of the company, you may be able to delay RMDs from that plan.
- **The Permanent Tax Window Advantage:**
  - Thanks to the **2025 One Big Beautiful Bill Act**, lower tax rates are permanent — giving you more flexibility to do gradual Roth conversions over multiple years without the pressure of a 2026 tax hike deadline.

Why This Matters for Retirees

- **Keeps Taxes Lower for Life:** Every dollar removed from your pre-tax balance before RMD age is one less dollar the IRS can force you to withdraw (and tax) later.
- **Protects Medicare Premiums:** Smaller RMDs mean a lower chance of IRMAA surcharges.
- **Preserves Tax-Free Growth:** Roth accounts can grow untouched for the rest of your life.
- **Improves Legacy Planning:** Heirs inherit Roth accounts tax-free, avoiding the 10-year depletion rule's tax burden.

Action Step

Complete the **RMD Eraser Worksheet**:

1. List all your pre-tax retirement accounts and their current balances.
2. Estimate your first RMD at age 73 or 75 using the IRS Uniform Lifetime Table.
3. Model how much smaller your RMD would be if you:
    - Converted a set amount to Roth annually between now and RMD age.
    - Used QCDs to offset part or all of your RMD after age 70½.
4. Pick **at least one** RMD-reduction strategy to start this year.

The Rationale (plain English)

1) RMDs are forced income

- Pre-tax accounts (Traditional IRA/401(k)/403(b)/SEP/SIMPLE) eventually require **Required Minimum Distributions**—withdrawals you **must** take and report as **taxable income**, even if you don't need the cash.
- Early RMDs are roughly **~3–5%** of the prior year-end balance and the percentage **ratchets up** as you age.
- *Mini-math:* If your IRA is **$900,000**, a first-year RMD around **~4%** would be about **$36,000**. That $36k stacks on top of your other income and can cascade through multiple parts of your tax picture.

2) The chain reaction (why a "little" RMD feels big)

A larger RMD doesn't just raise income tax—it can set off **domino effects**:

- **Higher bracket exposure:** RMD dollars sit on top of other income, potentially nudging you into the next **marginal bracket**.
- **Medicare IRMAA:** Premium surcharges are based on **MAGI** with a **two-year lookback**. A bigger RMD today can raise premiums **two years from now**.
- **Social Security taxation:** More ordinary income can cause a larger **portion of your SS benefits to be taxable**.

- **Investment surtaxes/cliffs:** An RMD can push you over thresholds that increase **capital-gains taxes** or trigger the **Net Investment Income Tax (NIIT)**.
- *Result:* What looked like "just" a required withdrawal can become an outsized **total cost** once all the cliffs and phase-ins react.

3) Defuse it early (before RMDs begin)

- Use your **pre-RMD years**—often lower-income **bridge years**—to do **bracket-aware Roth conversions** and/or planned withdrawals.
- Every dollar moved out of pre-tax now is a dollar **not** included in your future RMD calculation.
- *Directional example:* Reducing a pre-tax balance by **$200,000** before RMD age trims a first-year RMD by roughly **~$8,000/year** (assuming ~4%)—and that smaller base keeps saving you **every year** thereafter.

4) Charitable pressure valve (QCDs at 70½+)

- If you give annually, **Qualified Charitable Distributions** let you transfer IRA dollars **directly to charity** once you're **70½+**.
- QCDs **count toward your IRA RMD** yet **do not increase MAGI**, which helps with both **tax** and **IRMAA** exposure.
- Important limits & rules apply (e.g., **no** QCDs to **DAFs** or private foundations; keep the charity's acknowledgment).
- *Practical pattern:* Use QCDs to cover the **first dollars** of your IRA RMD, then take any remainder in cash (with tailored withholding), and consider **separate** Roth conversions only **after** the RMD is satisfied.

5) Control the flow (so RMDs don't control you)

- **Source RMDs smartly:** Choose which account(s) to pull from based on fees, holdings, and rebalancing needs.
- **Cadence:** Elect **monthly or quarterly** RMD payments to smooth cash flow and avoid big year-end tax shocks.
- **Withholding:** Set **clean withholding** (or use safe-harbor estimated payments) so you don't face penalties—and avoid over-withholding that drags on your cash.
- **Keep buffers:** Maintain small buffers below **bracket tops** and **IRMAA tiers** so a surprise dividend or capital-gain distribution doesn't push you over a cliff.

Bottom line: RMDs are inevitable, but **how large** they are—and **how painful** they feel—isn't. Shrink the problem **before** it starts, use **QCDs** if you give, and run RMDs with a steady **cadence + withholding plan**. That turns a tax **trap** into a **manageable line item**.

Key Mechanics (what trips people up)

1) Which accounts aggregate (and which don't)

- **IRAs (Traditional/SEP/SIMPLE):** Figure each IRA's RMD, **add them up**, and you may take the **total** from **any one** (or a mix) of your IRAs.
  Example: IRA-A RMD $4k, IRA-B $6k → total $10k. You can take the full $10k from IRA-B alone.
- **403(b)s:** Similar to IRAs—calculate each 403(b)'s RMD, **aggregate**, and take from **any 403(b)**.
- **401(k)s / 457(b)s: No aggregation.** You must take the RMD **separately from each plan**.
  Pitfall: Rolling old 401(k)s to an IRA before RMD age can simplify life (but check fees/investments first).
- **Roth IRAs: No lifetime RMDs** for the original owner.
- **Roth employer plans (e.g., Roth 401(k)/403(b)):** Currently **no pre-death RMDs** for owners under recent law, but **confirm with your plan** (administrative timing varies; inherited accounts differ).

2) Sequence rule (critical in RMD years)

- In any year an RMD applies, you must **take the RMD first**. Only **amounts above** the RMD can be **converted to Roth**.
  Example: RMD = $18,000; you want to convert $30,000. First distribute the **$18,000** (taxable, or satisfy some/ all via QCD if eligible). Then you may convert **up to $30,000** more.

3) QCD ordering & paperwork (age 70½+)

- A **Qualified Charitable Distribution** must be a **direct transfer** from your **IRA** to the charity. You cannot take cash first and "call it" a QCD later.
- QCDs **count toward** your **IRA** RMD and **do not increase MAGI**, which helps with **IRMAA**.
- **Not allowed**: Donor-Advised Funds or private foundations. Keep the **acknowledgment letter** from the charity.
  Pattern: Do QCDs **early** in the year to cover the first dollars of your IRA RMD; take any remainder as cash (with withholding) and only then consider separate Roth conversions.

4) IRMAA & MAGI (why deductions don't always help)

- **IRMAA** uses **MAGI = AGI + tax-exempt interest** with a **two-year lookback**.
- **QCDs** lower **AGI/MAGI** because they're excluded from income.
- **Itemized charitable deductions** do **not** lower MAGI—great for income tax, **irrelevant** to IRMAA.
  Guardrail: Keep **$1k–$5k** of headroom under the next IRMAA tier.

5) Withholding & penalties (make penalties a non-issue)

- Aim to meet the IRS **safe harbor** so you avoid underpayment penalties:
  - Pay at least **100%** of last year's total tax (**110%** if prior-year AGI > $150k), **or**
  - Pay **90%** of this year's projected tax.
- **Trick that helps:** Withholding from IRA/plan distributions (including an RMD) is treated as if paid **evenly throughout the year**—so a **late-year** withholding adjustment can "catch you up."
- Prefer **0% withholding on Roth conversions** (pay the tax from cash) so **every dollar** lands in Roth; set withholding on **RMD cash** instead.

6) Inherited accounts (don't mix rules)

- Keep inherited IRAs/401(k)s **separate** from your own. Post-SECURE rules commonly require the account to be emptied within **10 years**; some beneficiaries also owe **annual** RMDs depending on circumstances (e.g., if decedent died after RBD, beneficiary type).
- Spouses have special options (treat as own, remain beneficiary, or roll over) with different RMD implications.
- Practical move: maintain a **separate checklist** and calendar for inherited accounts.

7) Mini-checklist (run before you pull the trigger)

- ☐ I know **which accounts aggregate** and which don't.
- ☐ In RMD years, I will **take RMD first**, then convert.
- ☐ If eligible (70½+), I'll execute **QCDs before** other IRA withdrawals.
- ☐ My plan keeps me **$2k–$5k** under bracket tops and **$1k–$5k** under the next **IRMAA** tier.
- ☐ **Withholding/estimates** meet safe harbor; I'll use **late-year withholding** if needed.
- ☐ Inherited accounts have their **own** schedule and rules.

Get these mechanics right once, and your RMD years run on rails—predictable cash flow, fewer surprise surcharges, and more growth compounding where it's **tax-free**.

Readiness Quiz (score quickly)

How to use: Read each item and mark **Yes = 1 point** if it's true **this year**. Tally your score and follow the guidance below.

1) I've identified my RMD start year and can estimate the first-year amount.

- **How to check:** Note your first RMD year and last year-end balances for each pre-tax account. Multiply your total by a ~**3–5%** starter rate (early RMD years are ~a few percent).

- **Say "Yes" if:** You can write, "Projected first RMD ≈ $_____."
- **Why it matters:** Knowing the size of the first RMD tells you how much **forced income** you'll need to absorb.
- **Mini-math:** $900,000 × 4% = **$36,000** (900,000 × 0.04 = 36,000).

2) I have bridge years left (pre-RMD) to keep doing bracket-fill Roth conversions.

- **How to check:** List the years between now and RMD start (and before Social Security if applicable).
- **Say "Yes" if:** You have **≥1 year** where you can convert within the **22%/24%** bracket while keeping an **IRMAA buffer**.
- **Why it matters:** Each conversion now **shrinks** the future RMD base.

3) I give to charity and can use QCDs (age 70½+) from IRAs.

- **How to check:** Are you **70½ or older** this year, and do you make annual charitable gifts?
- **Say "Yes" if:** You plan to send **$_____** directly IRA → charity to **satisfy part of your IRA RMD**.
- **Why it matters: QCDs** count toward IRA RMDs **without increasing MAGI**, helping **tax** and **IRMAA**.

4) My RMDs can be set to monthly/quarterly to smooth taxes/cash flow.

- **How to check:** Ask your custodian if they can automate the RMD in installments and apply withholding.
- **Say "Yes" if:** You can choose **monthly/quarterly** payments with your preferred withholding.
- **Why it matters:** Smoother cash flow, easier tax planning, fewer penalty surprises.

5) I know which account(s) I'll tap to satisfy RMDs (and which to leave growing).

- **How to check:** Decide the source: which IRA/403(b) to satisfy from; remember **401(k) RMDs** must be taken **from each plan** separately.
- **Say "Yes" if:** You have a written **sourcing map** (e.g., "Satisfy IRA RMD from high-fee fund account; leave low-cost/desired holdings intact").
- **Why it matters:** Smart sourcing doubles as **portfolio cleanup** and keeps desired assets compounding.

6) My withholding/estimates meet safe-harbor rules.

- **How to check:** Compare year-to-date withholding + estimates against safe harbor:
  - Pay ≥ **100%** of last year's total tax (**110%** if prior-year AGI > $150k), **or**
  - Pay ≥ **90%** of this year's projected tax.
- **Say "Yes" if:** You meet a safe harbor or can adjust **RMD withholding** later in the year to catch up.
- **Why it matters:** Avoids underpayment **penalties**; late-year withholding on RMDs is treated as paid **evenly all year**.

7) My plan keeps me under IRMAA tiers with a small buffer.

- **How to check:** Estimate **MAGI = AGI + tax-exempt interest** after adding RMD (and any conversions). Compare to your IRMAA tier; keep **$1k–$5k** of headroom.
- **Say "Yes" if:** Your plan stays **below** the next tier with a buffer baked in.
- **Why it matters:** IRMAA uses a **two-year lookback**; today's misstep raises premiums later.

Score & Next Steps

0–2 → "Foundation first."

- Build your **RMD estimate**, list bridge years, and learn QCD basics.
- Ask custodian about **installment RMDs** and set a default withholding.

3–5 → "Build & pilot."

- Draft a **pre-RMD shrink plan** (bracket-fill conversions in bridge years).
- Set **monthly/quarterly** RMD cadence and a **QCD target** if 70½+.
- Confirm **safe-harbor** and **IRMAA** buffers with your CPA.

6–7 → "Document & automate."

- Lock your **sourcing map**, QCD amounts, and withholding percentages.
- Put **mid-year** and **Nov/Dec** reviews on the calendar; keep buffers.

Tie-Breakers (when you're on the fence)

- **Near an IRMAA cliff?** Favor **smaller** RMD cash and more **QCD** (IRA only) to protect MAGI.
- **Multiple 401(k)s?** Consider consolidating **before** RMD age (if appropriate) to simplify separate-plan RMDs.
- **Moving states?** Time conversions/RMD sourcing to the **lower-tax** state year.

One-Line Worksheet (fill now)

RMD start year	Est. first RMD $	Bridge years left	Planned conversions (per year) $	QCD target (70½+) $	RMD cadence
______	$________	______	$________	$________	☐ Mnthy ☐ Qrterly

RMD sourcing account(s)	Withholding plan	Safe harbor	IRMAA buffer after RMD $	Two-year lookback checked
______________________________	Fed __% / State __%	☐ Met ☐ Plan to adjust	$________	☐ Yes

Use this score as your green light: if you're in **3–7**, you're ready to run the Pillar-4 play—**shrink early, QCD where it fits, automate RMD flow, and protect buffers**.

Step-by-Step Implementation (10–15 minutes)

Goal: a pre-RMD **shrink strategy** + an **RMD-year checklist** you can run every year.
Minute 0–3 — Forecast the first-year RMD (ballpark)

- **Find your RMD start year.** Note the year you must begin RMDs for **each** pre-tax account type.
- **List all pre-tax balances** (Traditional IRA/SEP/SIMPLE, each 401(k)/403(b)/457(b) plan).
- **Estimate first-year RMD.** For a quick directional number, multiply your expected 12/31 balance by **~3–5%** (early RMD years are a few percent and increase over time).
    - *Mini-math:* $900,000 × 4% ≈ **$36,000**.
- **Write it down:** "Projected first-year RMD ≈ **$________**."

Tip: Do a second, conservative estimate using a **5%** factor to see a "stress-test" outcome.

Minute 4–6 — Map tax impact & cliffs

Add your **projected RMD** to this year's numbers and check three pressure points:

1. **Bracket top:**
    - Current projected **taxable income** + projected RMD = **new total**.
    - Will this push you over your target bracket? Leave a **$2k–$5k** cushion.

2. **IRMAA (two-year lookback):**
    - Compute **MAGI** (AGI + tax-exempt interest) with the RMD included.
    - Stay **$1k–$5k under** the next tier to avoid premium jumps later.
3. **Social Security taxation:**
    - Higher ordinary income usually increases the **taxable portion** of SS.
    - Note the directional change; you don't need exact decimals for planning.

One-line summary: "With RMD, I remain **$_____** under bracket top and **$_____** under the next IRMAA tier."

Minute 7–9 — Pre-RMD "shrink" tactics

Your objective is to **reduce** the future RMD base **before** it starts.

- **Bracket-fill Roth conversions (from Pillars 1–3):**
  Convert up to headroom in the **22%/24%** bracket with buffers.
    - *Playbook:* Larger conversions in **bridge years** (post-work, pre-SS/RMD); smaller after SS begins.
- **Harvest in down markets:**
  If the portfolio is off **10–15%**, use a **top-off conversion** so the rebound grows **tax-free** in Roth (stay under your buffers).
- **State-tax aware:**
  If you expect to **move** to a lower-tax state, consider **timing** conversions accordingly.
- **Charitable giver?**
  Plan to satisfy **future** IRA RMD dollars via **QCDs** once you're **70½+** (doesn't raise MAGI).

Minute 10–12 — RMD-year execution plan

Turn the "forced distribution" into a **predictable paycheck** with clean paperwork.

- **Cadence:**
  Set **monthly or quarterly** RMD payments to match spending and smooth withholding (avoids a big April bill).
- **Source (which account):**
  Decide which IRA/plan will satisfy the RMD:
    - Prefer accounts with **higher fees**, **overweight positions**, or holdings you plan to prune (RMD doubles as a rebalance).
    - Remember: **401(k)/457(b) RMDs must be taken from each plan separately**; IRAs and 403(b)s have their own aggregation rules.
- **QCD plan (if 70½+):**
  Decide $_____ to send **directly IRA → charity early in the year**; it **counts toward IRA RMD** and **doesn't increase MAGI**. Keep the charity's acknowledgment.

- **Withholding:**
  Set **federal/state** % on RMD installments **or** plan an **estimated payment** to satisfy safe-harbor rules.
    - *Tactic:* You can increase **late-year** RMD withholding; it's treated as if paid evenly all year.
- **Conversions in an RMD year:**
  Take the RMD first, then consider **additional** amounts as a **Roth conversion** (never convert the RMD itself).

Minute 13–15 — Paperwork & calendar
Make it repeatable and audit-proof.

- **Confirmations & tax docs:**
    - Save custodian confirmations for **RMDs** and **QCDs**.
    - Collect **1099-R** (distributions) and QCD acknowledgment letters in your tax folder.
- **Calendars (set recurring):**
    - **Mid-year review (May/June):** Update YTD income; adjust remaining RMD/QCD/withholding; recheck IRMAA buffer.
    - **Year-end (Nov/Dec):** Verify RMD **fully satisfied**; top-off **QCD** if needed; check for **capital-gain distributions** in taxable funds before any late moves; rebalance portfolio.
- **Contingency note:**
  If you realize an RMD was **missed**, contact your custodian/CPA promptly to correct—acting quickly often helps resolve penalties.

One-page worksheet (fill now)

RMD start year	Est. first RMD $	Bracket buffer after RMD $	IRMAA buffer after RMD (MAGI) $	Pre-RMD shrink this year (Roth conv) $	Buffers kept?	RMD cadence
______	$________	$________	$________	$________	☐ Yes	☐ Mthly ☐ Qrtly

Start date	RMD source account(s)	QCD target (70½+) $	QCD timing	Charity / EIN
____	______________________________ ____________	$______	________	________

Withholding — Fed %	Withholding — State %	Safe harbor	Mid-year review	Year-end verify
__%	__%	☐ Met ☐ Plan to adjust	____	____

Notes: ____

Done = you know **how big** the RMD will be, **where** it lands on your taxes/IRMAA, **how** you'll shrink the base ahead of time, and **how** you'll run RMDs each year (cadence, source, QCD, withholding) with clean documentation.

Real-World Examples (short & practical)

Numbers are **illustrative**. Plug in your bracket tops, IRMAA tiers, and state taxes before acting.

1) Bridge-year shrink — ***Elena (66), no SS yet***

- **Plan:** Convert **$45,000/yr** for **two years** (bridge years) → total **$90,000** shifted to Roth.
- **Directional RMD impact:** If the first RMD factor is ~4%, trimming the pre-tax base by **$90,000** reduces the first RMD by ≈ **$3,600** (0.04 × 90,000 = **3,600**).
- **Why it works:** Bridge years often have wide headroom (no wages, no SS). She fills the **22%** bracket with a **$2k–$5k** buffer under both the **bracket top** and **IRMAA** tier.

- **Tax ballpark (federal):** $45,000 × 22% = **$9,900** per year (plus any state tax), paid **from cash** (0% withholding on the conversion).
- **Paperwork:** Custodian confirmation now; **1099-R** and **5498** after year-end; **Form 8606** if IRA **basis** exists.

2) RMD + QCD combo – *Marcus (73), charitable giver*

- **Facts:** IRA **RMD = $22,000**. He gives to charity annually and is **70½+**.
- **Move:** Do a **QCD of $12,000** (IRA → charity **directly**) in February; remaining **$10,000** of the RMD is taken as **cash** with withholding.
- **Why it works:** The **$12,000 QCD satisfies** part of the IRA RMD but **does not increase MAGI**, protecting **IRMAA**. Only the **$10,000** cash distribution hits AGI/MAGI.
- **Withholding tactic:** Put most withholding on the **$10,000** cash piece (e.g., Fed __%, State __%) to meet **safe harbor**; keep **conversions** (if any) at **0% withholding**.
- **Must-dos:** Charity **acknowledgment** letter; QCD **cannot** go to a **DAF** or private foundation.

3) Plan-by-plan rule – *Avery (74) with multiple plans*

- **Accounts:** Two **401(k)s**, one **403(b)**, and two **IRAs**.
- **RMD mechanics:**
  - **Each 401(k)** → take **its own** RMD **separately**.
  - **403(b)s** → can aggregate **among 403(b)s**.
  - **IRAs (Traditional/SEP/SIMPLE)** → aggregate and take from **any one IRA**.
- **Execution:** Avery takes both 401(k) RMDs from each plan, aggregates the **IRA RMD** and pulls it entirely from the **high-fee IRA** he wants to downsize—solving taxes **and** portfolio cleanup in one move.
- **Optional simplifier (future years):** Consider consolidating old 401(k)s **before** RMD age when possible; once RMD age hits, special rollover sequencing rules apply (and each plan's RMD still must be satisfied).

4) After-RMD conversion – *Gina (74)*

- **Facts: RMD = $18,000**. She also wants to add to Roth **this year** without breaking buffers.
- **Sequence (critical):**
  1. Distribute **$18,000 RMD first** (cannot be converted).
  2. Then convert **$20,000 in-kind** to Roth with **0% withholding**, paying tax from **cash**.

- **Bracket/IRMAA check:** CPA confirms the RMD + **$20,000** conversion still keeps her **$2k–$5k** below both the **bracket top** and **IRMAA** tier.
- **Tax ballpark (federal):** $20,000 × 22% = **$4,400** (plus state, if any).
- **Paperwork:** Expect **1099-R** for both the RMD and the conversion distribution; **5498** for the Roth receipt; **Form 8606** as applicable.

Common guardrails across all four

- Leave **$2k–$5k** under your **target bracket** and **$1k–$5k** under the next **IRMAA** tier.
- Prefer **in-kind** conversions and **0% withholding** on conversions; place withholding on **RMD cash** to satisfy safe harbor.
- For IRA givers **70½+**, use **QCDs early** in the year to cover the first dollars of RMD **without raising MAGI**.
- Save confirmations and keep a tax folder for **1099-R**, **5498**, and QCD acknowledgments.

Mini Case Story — "RMD without the premium spike"

Bill (72) & Cara (70)

- **Profile:** Married filing jointly. Bill's first **RMD** is next year. Cara turns **70½** this year and gives to charity annually.
- **Goal:** Keep total income **below the next IRMAA tier**, avoid increasing the **taxable portion of Social Security**, and keep more growth compounding **tax-free**.

Year −1 (this year) — Use the last bridge year

- **Move: Roth convert $40,000, in-kind, 0% withholding** (taxes paid from cash).
- **Why now:** With no RMD yet, headroom in the **22% bracket** is widest. They leave a **$3k buffer** under the bracket top and **$2k** under the next IRMAA tier.
- **Directional tax:** $40,000 × 22% = **$8,800** federal (plus any state).
- **Effect:** Shrinks Bill's pre-tax balance **before** the first RMD is calculated.

Guardrails: Confirm Form 8606 as needed; save custodian confirmation; set calendar reminders for **mid-year** and **Nov/Dec** true-up.
Year 0 (RMD begins) — Sequence, charity, cash flow

1) Project & sequence

- **Projected RMD:** ≈ **$19,000** (directional).
- **Rule:** Take **RMD first**; only amounts above that can be **converted**.

2) QCD first (Cara 70½+)

- **Action: $8,000 QCD** from Bill's IRA **directly to charities** in **March**.
- **Impact:** Counts toward IRA RMD **without increasing MAGI**, protecting **IRMAA**. *(QCD cannot go to a DAF or private foundation.)*
- **Paperwork:** Charity acknowledgment letter; custodian's QCD confirmation.

3) Smooth the rest of the RMD

- **Remaining RMD: $11,000** (19,000 − 8,000).
- **Cadence:** Pay **monthly**: ~**$916.67**/mo (11,000 ÷ 12).
- **Withholding: 12% federal** from each monthly RMD → total annual withholding **$1,320** (11,000 × 0.12). This helps meet **safe harbor** without shrinking any Roth conversion.
- **Why monthly:** Matches cash needs, avoids a big April tax hit, and lets them adjust withholding late in the year if needed (withholding is treated as paid evenly all year).

4) After RMD, add a measured conversion

- **Action: Roth convert $10,000** more in late summer, **in-kind**, **0% withholding**; pay tax from cash.
- **Directional tax:** $10,000 × 22% = **$2,200** (plus state).
- **Check:** CPA confirms they remain **$2k–$3k below** both the target **bracket top** and the next **IRMAA** tier even after the conversion.

Why this works (the chain reaction managed)

- **IRMAA:** The **$8k QCD** satisfies part of the RMD **without** raising MAGI, keeping them under the next IRMAA tier.
- **Social Security taxation:** By capping MAGI, they avoid increasing the **taxable share** of SS.
- **Compounding:** The **$50k** moved to Roth across Year −1 and Year 0 (40k + 10k) now grows **tax-free**.
- **Future RMDs:** That same **$50k** reduction in pre-tax balances lowers future RMDs by roughly **~$2,000/yr** at a 4% factor (0.04 × 50,000 = **2,000**), and the savings recur annually.

Scripts they used (short & practical)
QCD instruction (custodian message):
"Please process a **Qualified Charitable Distribution** of **$8,000** from my IRA to **[Charity, EIN]** via direct transfer. Email written confirmation (amount, date)."
RMD setup (custodian message):

"Set my **remaining RMD** of **$11,000** to distribute **monthly** with **12% federal withholding** starting **[mm/dd]**. Email confirmation (schedule, withholding)."

Post-RMD conversion (custodian message):

"Convert **$10,000** from Traditional IRA to Roth IRA **in-kind** with **0% withholding**. Send written confirmation (date, amount, positions)."

Paper trail & calendar (so it's repeatable)

- **Save:** QCD confirmation + charity acknowledgment; RMD schedule letter; conversion confirmation; year-end **1099-R** and **5498**.
- **Calendar:**
  - **May/June:** Mid-year income check; adjust withholding if needed.
  - **November:** Verify total RMD satisfied; confirm IRMAA buffer still intact; consider no more conversions if buffer is tight.
  - **December:** Rebalance; ensure all confirmations filed.

Outcome (directional)

- **Premiums:** Stay **below** the next IRMAA tier (two-year lookback protected).
- **Taxes:** SS taxation **unchanged**; bracket **not breached** (buffers kept).
- **Portfolio: Roth grows**; **pre-tax base** smaller heading into Year 1 and beyond.
- **Process:** A clear, repeatable play for every RMD year: **QCD → remainder RMD on a cadence with withholding → (if safe) measured conversion.**

Note: Numbers are illustrative. Use your actual bracket tops, IRMAA tiers, and CPA-confirmed projections before executing.

Pro Tips, Scripts & Shortcuts

Use these copy-paste blocks, plus quick checklists, to lock in an RMD/QCD system that's clean, IRMAA-safe, and repeatable.

1) Email to CPA — RMD & QCD setup

Subject options (pick one):

- RMD/QCD plan + withholding check (bracket & IRMAA safe)
- Finalize this year's RMD cadence, QCD amount, and safe-harbor

Body (copy/paste):
Hi [Name] — I'd like to finalize my RMD plan for 20__.

Year (20__)	Estimated RMD $	Source accounts (pay from)	Proposed QCD $ (70½+)	QCD Charity / EIN
______	$____	[list accounts]	$____	

Remaining RMD $ (Est − QCD)	Payout cadence	Withholding — Fed %	Withholding — State %
$____	☐ Monthly ☐ Quarterly	__%	__%

Please confirm: 1) This keeps me under my target bracket and below the next IRMAA tier with a ~$[1–5]k buffer. 2) Safe-harbor status and whether I should adjust withholding or make an estimate. 3) Any state-tax nuances and the current QCD annual limit. 4) If I plan a Roth conversion after the RMD, how much is still "safe" this year? Attachments: account list & balances, last year's return (1040), YTD income/withholding. Thanks!

Follow-up nudge (if no reply in 3 biz days):
Just checking on my RMD/QCD plan — I'd like to start distributions on [date]. Can you confirm the amounts and withholding so I stay under bracket/IRMAA?

2) Custodian call / secure message — set automatic RMD
Phone script:
Please set my RMD from account ending [xxxx] to distribute $[amount] [monthly/quarterly], with [__% federal / __% state] withholding starting [mm/dd]. Email written confirmation showing the schedule, withholding percentages, and first payment date.
Secure message (same content):
RMD setup request — account [xxxx] Amount: $[amount] Cadence: [monthly/quarterly] Withholding: [__% federal / __% state] Start: [mm/dd] Please confirm in writing. Thank you.
What to have ready: bank link on file, preferred day of month, and whether you want **proportional liquidation** or from **specific positions** (often use RMD to prune high-fee or overweight holdings).

3) Custodian call / secure message — process a QCD (IRA only, age 70½+)
Phone script:
I want to make a Qualified Charitable Distribution of $[amount] from my IRA directly to [Charity Legal Name, EIN, mailing address]. Please confirm the check/wire instructions and send written confirmation.
Charity email (to request the right acknowledgment):
Subject: IRA Qualified Charitable Distribution — Acknowledgment Request Hello — I'm directing a Qualified Charitable Distribution of $[amount] from my IRA. Please provide a written acknowledgment stating the date, amount received, your EIN, and that no goods or services were provided in exchange. Thank you.
QCD essentials: direct IRA→charity transfer, keep the acknowledgment, not to DAFs/private foundations, confirm current annual QCD limits with your CPA.
4) Optional: Post-RMD Roth conversion (same year)
One-liner to custodian (after RMD is satisfied):
Convert $[amount] from Traditional IRA to Roth IRA in-kind with 0% withholding. Please confirm date, amount, and positions moved.
Guardrail: In an RMD year, **take the RMD first**; only **amounts above** it can be converted.

5) Guardrails (print at the top of your worksheet)

- **Sequence:** RMD → (optional) Roth conversion. Never convert the RMD itself.
- **QCDs:** IRA only; **direct transfer**; keep acknowledgment letters.
- **Buffers:** Leave **$2k–$5k** under your bracket top and **$1k–$5k** under the next IRMAA tier.
- **Withholding:** Meet **safe-harbor** via RMD withholding or estimates; remember late-year withholding is treated as paid evenly all year.
- **Aggregation rules:** IRAs & 403(b)s have their own aggregation; each **401(k)** RMD must be taken **from that plan**.
- **Docs:** Save confirmations; expect **1099-R** (distributions) and **5498** (Roth). Flag QCDs for your preparer (1099-R won't "label" them).

6) Quick FAQs (timely pitfalls)

- **Can I do a QCD from a 401(k)?** Generally **no** — QCDs are from **IRAs**. (Some roll to IRA first; coordinate timing with your CPA.)
- **I already took IRA cash — can I call it a QCD?** No. QCD must be **direct** IRA→charity.
- **Missed part of my RMD?** Contact custodian/CPA immediately to correct; ask about proper steps to address penalties if applicable.

- **Will the 1099-R show QCD?** It typically shows a normal distribution. Your **tax preparer** needs the QCD amount + acknowledgment letter to report correctly.

7) One-minute audit-proofing checklist

- ☐ RMD schedule letter saved (amount, cadence, withholding).
- ☐ QCD confirmation + charity acknowledgment on file.
- ☐ Post-RMD conversion confirmation (if done).
- ☐ Year-end: **1099-R** and **5498** collected; Form **8606** if needed.
- ☐ Calendar: **mid-year** review and **Nov/Dec** "RMD satisfied?" check.

8) Filled-in example snippets (illustrative)

- **CPA email lines:** "RMD $19,000; QCD $8,000; remaining $11,000 monthly with **12%** federal withholding; confirm bracket/IRMAA buffers remain ≥ **$2,000**."
- **Custodian RMD setup:** "$11,000 annual, **monthly** on the 15th, **12%** federal withholding; start **03/15**."
- **QCD instruction:** "$8,000 to **City Food Bank**, EIN **12-3456789**, 123 Main St, City, ST 00000."

These templates keep the moving parts straight: you satisfy RMDs **on rails**, use **QCDs** to protect MAGI/IRMAA, and (when appropriate) add a **measured conversion**—all with proof in your files.

Tools & Printables You'll Use

1) RMD Forecaster (one-pager)
Purpose: See the size of the problem, the tax ripple effects, and your remaining buffers at a glance.

How to fill: Use last Dec 31 balances (or your best year-end estimate), multiply by an **approx. RMD %** (early years ~3–5%), then layer in AGI/MAGI and buffers.

RMD FORECASTER (One-Pager)

Year	Est. Dec 31 Balance $	Approx. RMD %	Est. RMD $	Adds to AGI?	IRMAA Buffer Left $
20__	$________	____%	$________	☐ Yes	$________
20__	$________	____%	$________	☐ Yes	$________
20__	$________	____%	$________	☐ Yes	$________

Notes (QCD / Withholding / Offsets)

QCD target $____________________; Fed WH __%; State __%

Plan smaller conversion (SS year)

____

Down-market? consider top-off Roth

Mini example (illustrative):
Balance $900,000 × 4% ≈ **$36,000** RMD; if IRMAA tier buffer is $4,000, you know how much room remains for any Roth top-off.

2) RMD Sourcing Map

Purpose: Decide **which account(s)** will satisfy each RMD and use it to prune fees/overweights while keeping preferred assets compounding.

RMD SOURCING MAP

Account Type	**Account Name (Last 4)**	**Aggregates?**	**Annual RMD $**	**Source Method**	**Holdings to Use / Prune**
Traditional IRA	Custodian A (1234)	Yes (IRAs)	$____	☐ Monthly ☐ Quarterly	Sell/prune: High-fee fund XYZ
Traditional IRA	Custodian B (5678)	Yes (IRAs)	$____	☐ Monthly ☐ Quarterly	Use cash sleeve
403(b)	Plan C (9012)	Yes (403b)	$____	☐ Monthly ☐ Quarterly	Proportional
401(k)	Former Plan D (3456)	No (per plan)	$____	☐ Monthly ☐ Quarterly	Sell legacy target fund

Fees/Notes

Keep ETF ABC

____

____

Must take from this plan

Notes:

- **IRAs** aggregate with IRAs; **403(b)s** aggregate with 403(b)s; **each 401(k)/457(b)** stands alone.
- Use RMD sourcing as a **rebalance event** (trim overweight, high-fee, or redundant holdings).

3) QCD Planner (age 70½+; IRA only)

Purpose: Get charitable dollars out **first**, keep **MAGI** lower, and satisfy IRA RMD.

QCD PLANNER

Charity	EIN	Target $	Timing (Mo/Day)	Transfer Method	Acknowledgment Received?	Notes
________	______	$______	__ / __	Check / Wire (IRA→Charity)	☐ Yes ☐ No	QCD counts toward IRA RMD
________	______	$______	__ / __	Check / Wire (IRA→Charity)	☐ Yes ☐ No	Not to DAF/private foundation

Checklist:

- ☐ Age **70½+** this calendar year
- ☐ **Direct** IRA→charity transfer (not 401k; not cash to you)
- ☐ Acknowledgment letter saved (no goods/services received)
- ☐ Enter QCD amount on tax organizer (1099-R won't "label" it)

4) Withholding Safe-Harbor Tracker

Purpose: Avoid penalties and keep cash flow smooth. Use RMD withholding to "catch up" if needed (treated as paid evenly through the year).

WITHHOLDING / SAFE HARBOR

PY Total Tax (Line 24) $	Safe Harbor Target (select one)	Safe Harbor Target $	TY Projected Tax (90%) $	YTD Withholding $	Estimated Payments $
$________	☐ 100% ☐ 110% (if PY AGI > $150k)	$________	$________	$________	$________

Gap to Target $	RMD Withholding – Fed %	RMD Withholding – State %	Additional Estimate – Q2 (__ /___ /20___)	Q3 (__ /___ /20___)	Q4 (__ /___ /20___)	Jan (__ /___ /20___)
$________	__%	__%	______	______	______	______

Dates (typical): Q1 Apr 15, Q2 Jun 15, Q3 Sep 15, Q4 Jan 15 (next year).

5) RMD-Year Checklist (one page)

Purpose: Run the same clean sequence every year.

RMD-YEAR CHECKLIST

Category	Item	Amount / Details	Done?
Sequencing	IRA QCD(s) executed first (70½+)	$________; direct transfer; acknowledgment letters saved	☐
Sequencing	Remaining IRA/403(b)/401(k) RMD scheduled & satisfied	$________	☐
Sequencing	Post-RMD Roth conversion considered (buffers kept)	$________	☐
Cliff & Tax Checks	Bracket buffer maintained	≥ $2k–$5k	☐
Cliff & Tax Checks	IRMAA buffer maintained (two-year lookback)	≥ $1k–$5k	☐
Cliff & Tax Checks	Social Security taxation impact reviewed	–	☐
Cliff & Tax Checks	Fund capital-gain distributions (taxable accts; often Dec) checked	–	☐
Cash & Paperwork	Cadence set	☐ Monthly ☐ Quarterly • Start: __ /___/20___	☐
Cash & Paperwork	Withholding set	Fed __% / State __%	☐
Cash & Paperwork	Safe harbor	☐ Met	☐
Cash & Paperwork	Confirmations saved (RMD/QCD/Conversion)	–	☐
Cash & Paperwork	1099-R / 5498 filed later	–	☐

6) Calendar Pack (recurring reminders)

Purpose: Make the plan automatic.

- **Mid-Year Review (May/June):** Update YTD income; reconfirm bracket & IRMAA buffers; adjust remaining RMD/QCD/withholding.
- **Year-End Verification (Nov/Dec):** Confirm **RMD fully satisfied**; scan for taxable **fund distributions**; finalize withholding; consider **small top-off conversion** only if buffers remain.
- **Monthly/Quarterly RMD cadence:** Set payment day; verify bank link.
- **QCD Deadline:** Block time early in the year (and again in November for any true-up).
- **"Room Shrinks" Flags:** 90-day alerts before **Social Security start** and **RMD start** years.
- **Tax Docs:** January—collect 1099-R/5498; confirm QCD acknowledgments in file.

Optional: "All-in-One" Summary Sheet (front page of the binder)

This Year at a Glance - Planned IRA

QCD $	**QCD date**	**Total RMD(s) $**	**Cadence**	**Withholding – Fed %**	**Withholding – State %**	**Post-RMD Roth $**
$________	__ /__ /20___	$________	☐ M ☐ Q	__%	__%	$________

Roth method	**Roth withholding**	**Bracket buffer $**	**IRMAA buffer $**	**Mid-Year review**	**Year-End verify**
In-kind	0%	$________	$________	__ /__ /20___	__ /__ /20___

Notes: ____

With these pages filled, your RMD years run on rails: **QCD first** (if eligible), **RMD on a cadence with clean withholding, optional measured conversion** only when buffers allow—tracked, documented, and calendar-driven.

Action Step (what to complete now)

Objective: leave this pillar with a written **RMD game plan** you can run on autopilot: a pre-RMD **shrink strategy**, an **RMD-year cash-flow + withholding** setup, an **optional QCD** play, and **calendar reminders**—so RMDs don't push you over tax or IRMAA cliffs.

1) Estimate your first-year RMD (write it down)

IRA (12/31 est.) $	401(k) (12/31 est.) $	403(b) (12/31 est.) $	Other (12/31 est.) $	Starter rate (early RMD ~3–5%)	Projected first-year RMD $
$____	$____	$____	$____	____%	$________

- *Quick check:* If balance is $800,000 and you use **4%**, RMD ≈ **$32,000** (800,000 × 0.04 = 32,000).

Note your buffers after adding the RMD:

- **Bracket buffer left:** $________
- **IRMAA buffer left (MAGI):** $________

2) Pick a pre-RMD shrink move (this year)

Roth conversion $ (with buffers)	Method	Withholding	Taxes paid from	Market-dip trigger	State-tax note (if moving)
$________	In-kind	0%	Cash	"If portfolio −__%, **convert up to $____** (within buffers)."	____________________

3) Decide RMD cadence and source account

Cadence	Start date	Account(s) that will satisfy RMD
☐ Monthly ☐ Quarterly	__ /___ /20___	____________________________

- (Prefer accounts with higher fees/overweights you want to prune.)

4) Set QCD amount (if age 70½+) — IRA only

QCD this year $	Month	Charity / EIN	Custodian directions requested?	Acknowledgment letter saved?
$________	__________	______________________________	☐ Yes ☐ No	☐ Yes ☐ Pending

Remember: QCD = **direct** IRA→charity, counts toward **IRA** RMD, **doesn't increase MAGI**, not allowed to DAFs/private foundations.

5) Lock withholding / estimates to meet safe harbor

Safe-harbor target (select one)	RMD withholding — Fed %	State %	Additional estimates — Q2 (__ /___ /20___)	Q3 (__ /___ /20___)	Q4 (__ /___ /20___)	Jan (__ /___ /20___)
☐ 100% prior-year ☐ 110% (if PY AGI > $150k) ☐ 90% current-year	__%	__%	______	______	______	______

Tip: Late-year RMD withholding is treated as paid **evenly all year**—use it to "catch up."

6) Email your CPA and set your calendar

- **Send plan summary** (copy/paste):

Subject: RMD/QCD plan and withholding check Hi [Name] — Please confirm my plan keeps me under my target bracket and below the next IRMAA tier with a ~$[1–5]k buffer. • Est. RMD this year: $____ from [accounts] • QCD (70½+): $____ from IRA directly to [Charity, EIN] • RMD cadence: [monthly/quarterly], withholding [__% federal / __% state] • Post-RMD Roth conversion (if safe): $____ (in-kind, 0% withholding) Also confirm safe-harbor status and any state-tax nuances. Thanks!

- **Calendar**
  - **Mid-Year Review (May/June):** update YTD income; adjust remaining RMD/QCD/withholding; recheck IRMAA.
  - **Year-End (Nov/Dec):** verify **RMD fully satisfied**; scan for **mutual-fund distributions** in taxable accts; top-off QCD if needed; rebalance.
  - **Doc day (January):** collect **1099-R**, **5498**, and QCD acknowledgments.

One-Page Worksheet (fill now)

RMD start year	Est. first RMD $	Bracket buffer $ (post-RMD)	IRMAA buffer (MAGI) $ (post-RMD)	Pre-RMD Roth conversion $	Buffers kept?	Market-dip trigger (−% → +$)
______	$________	$________	$________	$________	☐ Yes	−% → +$______

RMD execution:

Cadence	Start date	Amount per pay $	Source account(s)	QCD $ (70½+)	QCD month	Charity / EIN
☐ Monthly ☐ Quarterly	—	$________	______________________________ ______________________________	$______	____	________________

Custodian instructions sent?	Acknowledgment saved?	Withholding — Fed %	Withholding — State %	OR estimate dates	Safe harbor	Adjust by (date)	CPA email sent	Mid-Year review	Year-End verify
☐ Yes ☐ No	☐ Yes	__%	__%	________	☐ Met ☐ Will adjust	_	__	__	__

Notes: ____

Quick Example (illustrative math)

- **Est. first RMD:** Balance $800,000 × 4% = **$32,000**.
- **QCD:** $5,000 IRA→charity (counts toward the $32,000; **no MAGI hit**).
- **Remaining RMD:** $32,000 − $5,000 = **$27,000**.
  - **Monthly cadence:** $27,000 ÷ 12 = **$2,250** per month.
  - **Withholding:** 12% of $27,000 = **$3,240** for the year (0.12 × 27,000 = 3,240) → **$270** withheld per month (3,240 ÷ 12 = 270).
- **Post-RMD Roth conversion (if buffers allow):** $10,000, in-kind, **0% withholding**, tax from cash.

"Done" Checklist

- ☐ First-year RMD estimated; bracket/IRMAA impact noted
- ☐ Pre-RMD shrink amount chosen (with buffers)
- ☐ RMD cadence & source account set; instructions ready
- ☐ QCD amount set (if 70½+); custodian directions requested; ack letter plan in place
- ☐ Withholding/estimates aligned to safe harbor
- ☐ CPA emailed; mid-year & Nov/Dec reviews scheduled

Deliverable: your written **RMD game plan**—pre-RMD shrink strategy, RMD-year cash-flow + withholding, optional QCD, and calendar reminders—so RMDs are predictable and **IRMAA-safe**, not a tax ambush.

Pillar 4 — Executive Summary

Introduction & Key Points

- **Problem:** RMDs are **forced, taxable income** that can push you over **tax brackets**, **IRMAA** tiers, and increase **Social Security taxation**.
- **Strategy:** Shrink the pre-tax balance **before** RMDs start, then run RMDs on **rails**: QCDs first (if eligible), the rest on a **monthly/quarterly cadence** with clean **withholding**, and (only if safe) a **post-RMD Roth conversion**.
- **Outcome:** Lower lifetime taxes, fewer premium surprises, steadier cash flow.

The Rationale (plain English)

- RMD % starts around ~**3–5%** and rises, creating a **chain reaction** across taxes and benefits.
- **Pre-RMD conversions** cut the future base; **QCDs** satisfy IRA RMD **without raising MAGI**; good **withholding** turns the "tax trap" into a predictable bill.

Key Mechanics (what trips people up)

- **Aggregation rules:** IRAs aggregate with IRAs; **403(b)s** with 403(b)s; each **401(k)/457(b)** stands alone. **Roth IRAs** have no lifetime RMDs.
- **Sequence:** In an RMD year, **take the RMD first**, then convert any **extra**.
- **QCDs: Direct IRA→charity**, age **70½+**; not to DAFs; keeps **MAGI** lower.
- **IRMAA:** Two-year lookback on **MAGI**; itemized deductions don't help MAGI.
- **Withholding:** Meet **safe-harbor** via RMD withholding or estimates; late-year withholding counts as if paid all year.
- **Inherited accounts:** Separate rules and timing—keep them distinct.

Readiness Quiz (score quickly)

- 7 yes/no items on: RMD start & estimate, bridge-year conversions, QCD eligibility, cadence, sourcing, safe-harbor, IRMAA buffer.
- **0–2:** Build estimates + QCD basics
- **3–5:** Pre-RMD shrink + cadence
- **6–7:** Document & automate.

Step-by-Step Implementation (10–15 minutes)

1. **Forecast** first-year RMD and note bracket/IRMAA buffers.
2. **Map impact:** bracket top, IRMAA tier, SS taxation.
3. **Pre-RMD shrink:** bracket-fill conversions; use market dips; consider state-tax timing.
4. **RMD year plan:** set **monthly/quarterly** cadence, choose source account(s), **QCD first**, then (if safe) a measured **conversion**; set **withholding**.

5. **Paperwork & calendar:** confirmations, 1099-R/5498, mid-year review, Nov/Dec verify.

Real-World Examples (short & practical)

- **Elena (66):** $45k/yr ×2 conversions → trims first RMD by ≈ **$3,600**; stays under IRMAA.
- **Marcus (73):** RMD $22k; **QCD $12k** + $10k cash RMD with withholding → lower MAGI.
- **Avery (74):** Takes each **401(k)** RMD separately; aggregates **IRAs** from a high-fee account.
- **Gina (74):** RMD $18k first, then **$20k** conversion—buffers intact.

Mini Case Story — "RMD without the premium spike"

- **Bill (72) & Cara (70):**
  - **Year −1:** Convert **$40k** (buffers kept).
  - **Year 0:** RMD ≈ **$19k** → **QCD $8k**, remaining **$11k** monthly with **12%** withholding; then **$10k** conversion.
  - **Result:** IRMAA avoided, SS taxation steady, Roth grows, pre-tax base shrinks.

Pro Tips, Scripts & Shortcuts

- **CPA email:** confirm RMD/QCD amounts, bracket & IRMAA buffers, safe-harbor status, and any post-RMD conversion room.
- **Custodian scripts:** set **automatic RMD** cadence with withholding; issue **QCD** (direct transfer); confirm **post-RMD conversion**.
- **Guardrails:** RMD → (optional) conversion; QCDs **direct**; keep **$2–5k** under bracket top and **$1–5k** under next IRMAA tier.

Tools & Printables You'll Use

- **RMD Forecaster**, **RMD Sourcing Map**, **QCD Planner (70½+)**, **Withholding Safe-Harbor Tracker**, **RMD-Year Checklist**, **Calendar Pack** (mid-year review, Nov/Dec verify, cadence, QCD deadline).

Action Step (what to complete now)

- Write your **RMD estimate** and buffers; choose a **pre-RMD conversion**; set **cadence & source**; set **QCD** (if 70½+); lock **withholding/estimates**; email **CPA**; schedule **mid-year** and **Nov/Dec** checks.
- **Deliverable:** a written **RMD game plan** that keeps you under **brackets** and **IRMAA** cliffs while growing more in **tax-free** accounts.

Educational only; not tax advice. Coordinate specifics with a qualified tax professional.

Pillar 5 — Tax-Free Legacy Planning

Introduction and Key Points

You've worked hard to lower lifetime taxes. Now the goal is to make sure what you leave behind is **simple, fast, and as tax-free as possible** for the people and causes you care about. This pillar turns complex estate and beneficiary rules into a clear plan that:

- steers heirs toward **Roth** and other **tax-advantaged** dollars,
- uses **step-up in basis** where it helps (taxable accounts),
- avoids avoidable taxes, penalties, and probate delays, and
- keeps your wishes honored with clean, current paperwork.

Why this matters
Most non-spouse heirs must empty inherited IRAs/401(k)s within **10 years** under current rules. That can spike their taxes in peak earning years—unless you **design the inheritance** (Roth first, smart beneficiary splits, or charitable carve-outs). Meanwhile, **taxable accounts** may receive a **step-up in basis** at death (rules vary), making them attractive to pass as-is. Getting the **right asset to the right heir** is the difference between a smooth gift and a costly surprise.

What we'll do in this module

- Map which accounts heirs should receive **and why** (Roth vs. pre-tax vs. taxable).
- Clean up **beneficiary designations** (primary/contingent, **per stirpes**, TOD/POD) and align them with your will/trust.
- Build a **10-year game plan** for inherited retirement accounts (spouse vs. non-spouse options, timing to avoid bracket spikes).
- Add **charitable tools** (QCDs now, charity as IRA beneficiary later) to keep MAGI lower for you and taxes lower for heirs.
- Create a one-page **Legacy Brief** your executor and family can follow without guesswork.

What to have handy

- A current **account list by type** (Traditional/SEP/SIMPLE IRA, 401(k)/403(b), Roth IRA/401(k), taxable, HSA).
- **Beneficiary forms** for each account (who's primary, who's contingent, percentages).

- Your **estate documents** (will/trust/POAs) and any charitable intentions.
- A short list of heirs with approximate **tax situations** (e.g., high earner vs. lower earner).

Your outcome

By the end of Pillar 5 you'll have a **tax-smart inheritance map**: clear beneficiaries per account, a plan to favor **tax-free** inheritances where it counts, a simple timeline heirs can follow (including the 10-year clock for inherited retirement accounts), and annual reminders to keep everything up to date. *(Educational, not legal/tax advice—loop in your attorney/CPA to finalize.)*

Key Points

- **The SECURE Act's 10-Year Rule:**
  - Most non-spouse heirs must fully withdraw inherited IRA/401(k) funds within **10 years**, creating a large, taxable income spike.
  - This can push heirs into much higher tax brackets during peak earning years.
- **Why Roth Accounts Solve This:**
  - Roth IRAs still follow the 10-year depletion rule for non-spouse heirs, but **withdrawals are tax-free**.
  - No taxable income means no bracket jumps for your beneficiaries.
- **Beneficiary Designations Matter:**
  - Always update beneficiary forms after major life events (marriage, divorce, birth, death).
  - Ensure you list *primary* and *contingent* beneficiaries—wills and trusts don't override retirement account forms.
- **Trust Planning for Complex Situations:**
  - If leaving assets to minors, special needs heirs, or those who may mismanage funds, consider a trust that holds Roth assets and distributes under set rules.
- **Gifting Strategies While Alive:**
  - Gradual gifting to heirs or funding their Roth IRAs while you're alive can shift future growth out of your estate and into tax-free vehicles sooner.
- **OBBBA Advantage:**
  - With lower tax rates made permanent under the **2025 One Big Beautiful Bill Act**, you can complete Roth conversions over several years without a looming tax hike deadline—maximizing the tax-free portion of your estate.

Why This Matters for Retirees

- **Preserves More Wealth for Your Family:** Reduces the share that goes to taxes upon your passing.
- **Avoids Unintended Tax Burdens:** Prevents heirs from facing surprise multi-thousand-dollar tax bills.
- **Provides More Control:** Trusts and proper designations let you dictate how and when heirs access funds.
- **Maximizes the Permanent Low-Tax Window:** Every Roth dollar converted now is a future tax-free dollar for your heirs.

Action Step

Complete the **Beneficiary Blueprint Checklist**:

1. Review all retirement and investment accounts to confirm **primary and contingent beneficiaries** are accurate.
2. Decide if certain heirs would benefit from **inherited Roth IRAs** instead of taxable accounts.
3. If needed, consult an estate attorney about **trust structures** for minors, special needs heirs, or spendthrift beneficiaries.
4. Set a 3–5 year **Roth conversion plan** to maximize tax-free legacy assets while rates are permanently low.

The Rationale (plain English)

1) Different buckets = different tax fates

- **Roth dollars (best for high-tax heirs):**
  Heirs generally must empty inherited **Roth** accounts within **10 years**, but withdrawals are **income-tax-free** if the original owner's **5-year Roth clock** has been met.
    - *What the clock means:* If **any** Roth IRA of the original owner has been open for **5 tax years**, beneficiaries can withdraw both principal **and earnings** tax-free during their 10-year window. If not, **earnings** may be taxable until that 5-year mark is reached (contributions/conversions are still available tax-free first).
    - *Design tip:* Favor leaving **Roth** to **high-income** heirs—they get the biggest benefit from tax-free withdrawals.
- **Pre-tax IRA/401(k) dollars (usually worst for high-tax heirs):**
  Inherited **pre-tax** accounts create **ordinary taxable income** as heirs withdraw. For non-spouse heirs, most must empty the account within **10 years**, often during peak earning years.

    - *Mini-math:* If your child in the 35% bracket withdraws **$100,000** from an inherited IRA, they might owe **$35,000** federal tax (plus state). Spreading withdrawals across several years can reduce bracket spikes.
    - *Design tip:* Consider steering more **pre-tax** dollars to **lower-income** heirs **or** to **charity**.
- **Taxable (brokerage) accounts (step-up potential):**
  Many taxable assets receive a **step-up in basis** at death—cost basis resets to date-of-death value—potentially erasing embedded capital gains for heirs.
    - *Mini-math:* If you bought stock for **$50,000** now worth **$140,000**, a full step-up makes the heir's basis **$140,000**; selling at **$142,000** triggers gains on just **$2,000**.
    - *Nuance:* Community-property states, joint ownership, and titling can change how much steps up. Confirm locally.

2) Design beats default

- **Beneficiary forms rule** retirement accounts (and often trump your will). Keeping **primary** and **contingent** beneficiaries current prevents probate delays and directs **who gets what, in which tax wrapper**.
- Add **per stirpes** if you want a beneficiary's share to flow to their children if they predecease you.
- Use **TOD/POD** on bank/brokerage accounts to pass outside probate while preserving step-up potential.

3) Charitable carve-outs multiply impact

- **Best asset to charity: Pre-tax IRA** dollars. A charity pays **no income tax**, so every dollar lands where you intend.
- Two simple paths:
    - Name a **charity** as **partial beneficiary** of your IRA (e.g., "20% to Charity, 80% to heirs").
    - During life (age **70½+**), use **QCDs** (IRA → charity **directly**) to reduce the IRA **without increasing your MAGI**, which can also help with **IRMAA**.
- Pair this with leaving **Roth** and **taxable** assets to family for better after-tax results.

4) Simplicity helps survivors

- In hard moments, the best gift is **clarity**. A one-page **Legacy Brief** with:
    - account list and **who inherits what**,
    - the **10-year rule** summary for inherited retirement accounts (and spouse options),

- contact info (custodians, advisor/CPA/attorney), and
- "First 30–60 days" steps

can save months of confusion and prevent costly mistakes (missed deadlines, wrong titling, avoidable taxes).

Bottom line: Put **Roth** where it's most valuable (high-tax heirs), send **pre-tax** where it hurts least (lower-tax heirs or **charity**), let **taxable** benefit from **step-up**, and make it all work smoothly with **clean beneficiary forms** and a plain-English **Legacy Brief**.

Key Mechanics (what trips people up)

1) Beneficiary forms control retirement accounts

- **They trump your will.** For IRAs/401(k)/403(b), the custodian pays whoever is on the **beneficiary form**—even if your will says otherwise.
- **Keep both layers current:**
  - **Primary + Contingent** (with percentages that sum to 100%).
  - Add **per stirpes** if you want a beneficiary's share to pass to **their children** if they predecease you (vs. per capita, which re-allocates among surviving peers).
- **Minors & special needs:**
  - Naming a **minor** directly can require a court-appointed guardian to receive assets. Prefer a **custodian (UTMA)** or a **trust**.
  - For heirs with disabilities, use a properly drafted **special needs trust** so benefits aren't jeopardized.
- **Proof:** Ask the custodian for a **beneficiary confirmation letter** after every change.

2) SECURE-era 10-year rule (most non-spouse heirs)

- **Most non-spouse "designated beneficiaries"** must empty inherited **IRA/Roth IRA** within **10 years** of death. There may be no annual RMD, but the **entire account must be zero by year 10** (rules vary by facts; get advice).
- **Eligible Designated Beneficiaries (EDBs)**—who may stretch over life expectancy—generally include:
  1. **Surviving spouse**
  2. **Minor child of the decedent** (until majority; then 10-year clock starts)
  3. **Disabled** individuals
  4. **Chronically ill** individuals
  5. A beneficiary **≤10 years younger** than the decedent
- **Spouse options (powerful):**
  - **Treat as own** (roll into spouse's IRA) → new owner's rules apply; RMDs based on spouse's age; Roth keeps owner benefits.

    - **Remain beneficiary** (inherited IRA) → can start/stop RMD timing strategically depending on ages.
- **Trusts need precision:** "**Conduit**" vs "**accumulation**" trusts produce very different payout and tax results; have an attorney review.

3) Roth details that matter

- **No lifetime RMDs** for owners. Inherited **Roth IRAs** are usually subject to the **10-year** emptying window.
- **5-year clock for tax-free earnings:** If **any Roth IRA** owned by the decedent has been open **5 tax years**, heirs' withdrawals of **earnings** are income-tax-free; if not, heirs may owe tax on earnings withdrawn before the clock is met.
- **Recordkeeping tip:** Keep the **original Roth start year** on your Legacy Brief so heirs don't guess.
- **Conversions vs. contributions:** The owner's 5-year **penalty** clocks (for early distributions) **don't apply** to beneficiaries; the relevant item for heirs is **tax-free earnings** after the 5-year **owner** clock.

4) HSA nuance (easy to get wrong)

- **Spouse beneficiary:** Can treat the HSA as **their own**—keeps its triple tax advantage.
- **Non-spouse beneficiary:** The HSA generally becomes **taxable income** in the year of death to the beneficiary.
    - Limited relief may apply for **the decedent's** unpaid qualified medical expenses if paid **within one year**—coordinate with a CPA.
- **Planning tip:** HSAs are usually best **spent during your lifetime** (qualified medical/Medicare premiums) rather than left to non-spouse heirs.

5) Taxable accounts & titling (step-up mechanics)

- **Step-up in basis** may reset cost basis to date-of-death value, reducing/erasing capital gains for heirs.
- **Titling changes outcomes:**
    - **Community property** often gets a **full** step-up;
    - **Joint tenancy** may get a **partial** step-up (only the decedent's portion);
    - **Tenancy by the entirety** varies—confirm locally.
- **TOD/POD** registrations can bypass probate and still preserve step-up—use with care to keep the plan coordinated with your will/trust.
- **Estate as beneficiary:** Often **worst** for taxes/timing; avoid unless counsel advises.

6) Coordination risk (the silent gotcha)

- **Mismatch** between beneficiary forms, TOD/POD, and your will/trust creates accidental disinheritance or tax drag.
- **When to review:** After **marriage, divorce, birth/adoption, death**, beneficiary moves, big asset changes, or new charitable goals—and **annually** as a habit.
- **Name roles clearly:** Executor/personal representative, successor trustee, and **backup** people; make sure they know **where documents live** and how to reach your **CPA/attorney/advisor**.

Mini-checklist (print this)

- ☐ Primary **and** contingent beneficiaries current (percentages total 100%)
- ☐ "**Per stirpes**" selected where desired
- ☐ Minor or special-needs heirs routed via appropriate **trust/custodian**
- ☐ **Roth** opened **>5 tax years**; start year documented
- ☐ **HSA**: spouse vs. non-spouse outcome understood; lifetime spend plan noted
- ☐ **Taxable** accounts titled correctly; **TOD/POD** used where appropriate
- ☐ **Charity** receives **pre-tax** slice (at death) or QCD plan (during life)
- ☐ Will/trust and beneficiary forms **match**; annual review date set

Readiness Quiz (score quickly)

How to use: Read each item and mark **Yes = 1 point** if it's true **today**. Tally your score and follow the guidance at the end.

1) My beneficiary forms (primary & contingent) match my wishes and list percentages.

- **How to check:** Download beneficiary confirmations from each custodian (IRA/401(k)/403(b)/Roth/HSA/annuity). Confirm **primary + contingent** sum to 100%; add **per stirpes** where desired.
- **Say "Yes" if:** All accounts have current names, percentages, and per-stirpes where needed.
- **If No (5-minute fix):** Request update links/forms; set a calendar reminder to submit this week.

2) I've mapped accounts to heirs by tax character
(Roth → high earners, Taxable → anyone, Pre-tax → lower earners/charity).

- **How to check:** Label each account **Roth / Pre-tax / Taxable / HSA** and match to heirs.

- **Say "Yes" if:** Your design consciously directs **Roth** to higher-bracket heirs, **pre-tax** to lower-bracket heirs or **charity**, and **taxable** wherever (step-up potential).
- **If No:** Draft a simple "who gets what" table; align beneficiary forms accordingly.

3) I understand the 10-year rule for non-spouse heirs (and spouse options).

- **How to check:** Can you summarize: "Most non-spouse heirs must empty inherited IRA/Roth within **10 years**; spouses can **treat as own**, **roll over**, or **remain beneficiary**"?
- **Say "Yes" if:** You could explain this to an heir in one sentence and know to ask your attorney about trusts (conduit vs. accumulation).
- **If No:** Add a one-paragraph explainer to your Legacy Brief.

4) I have at least one Roth open > 5 tax years to secure tax-free earnings for heirs.

- **How to check:** Note your **earliest Roth IRA open year**.
- **Say "Yes" if:** A Roth of yours has been open **≥5 tax years** (contributions or any amount) so beneficiaries can withdraw **earnings tax-free** during their 10-year window.
- **If No:** Open/fund a Roth IRA (even a small contribution/conversion) to **start the clock**; record the start year.

5) I have a QCD/charitable plan or IRA → charity beneficiary for part of pre-tax dollars.

- **How to check:** If **70½+**, list annual **QCD** amount (IRA→charity **direct**) that satisfies part of your IRA RMD without raising **MAGI**. If younger or planning at death, assign a **% of IRA to charity** as beneficiary.
- **Say "Yes" if:** You've chosen **either** QCD during life **or** named a charity to receive a slice of **pre-tax** at death.
- **If No:** Pick a small % or dollar target and add charity **EIN** to your sheet.

6) I maintain a one-page Legacy Brief (accounts, contacts, "what to do first").

- **How to check:** Do you have a single page with account list, custodian phone numbers, advisor/CPA/attorney contacts, and a **first 30–60 days** checklist?
- **Say "Yes" if:** It exists and is printable/shareable today.
- **If No:** Draft it now; perfection later.

7) My executor/trustee and key heirs know where these documents live.

- **How to check:** Have you told **at least two** trusted people where to find your Legacy Brief, will/trust/POAs, and beneficiary confirmations?

- **Say "Yes" if:** They know the **location** (and, if digital, how to access it).
- **If No:** Send a short "where to find things" email today.

Score & Next Steps

0–2 → Foundation first

- Update **beneficiaries** (primary/contingent/per stirpes).
- Create a one-page **Legacy Brief** and note your **Roth start year**.

3–5 → Optimize

- Map assets to heirs by **tax character**; start **QCD** plan (70½+) or set **IRA→charity** %.
- Add a 2-line **10-year rule** explainer to your Brief.

6–7 → Finalize & automate

- Send the **where-it-lives** email to executor/trustee + backup.
- Calendar an **annual review** (birthday month) and after major life events.

One-Line Worksheet (fill now)

Beneficiaries current?	Roth open year	≥5 tax years met?	Asset map — Roth →	Asset map — Pre-tax →	Charity % (from pre-tax)
☐ Yes	______	☐ Yes	______	______	____%

Asset map — Taxable →	10-year rule noted in Legacy Brief?	QCD (70½+) $/year or IRA→Charity
______	☐ Yes	$_______

Beneficiary % to charity	Charity name	Charity EIN	Legacy Brief done?	Document location
____%	__________	________	☐ Yes	__________________

Told executor/trustee + backup?	Names (exec/trustee / backup)	Annual review date (MM / DD)
☐ Yes	__________________ / __________________	__ / __

Done = you've locked the **who/what/where** so heirs inherit the **right assets**, minimize taxes, and avoid chaos.

Step-by-Step Implementation (10–15 minutes)

Goal: finalize **who gets what**, place assets in the **most tax-smart buckets**, and produce a clear **10-year play** your heirs can follow.

Minute 0–3 — Inventory & label by tax type

Create a fast snapshot so decisions are obvious.

Mini table (fill now):

Account / Custodian	Type (Roth / Pre-tax / Taxable / HSA)	Balance
Vanguard IRA	Pre-tax	$_____
Fidelity Roth IRA	Roth (open year: 20__)	$_____
Schwab Brokerage	Taxable	$_____
Bank HSA	HSA	$_____

Owner	Primary %	Contingent %	Per stirpes?	TOD/POD?
You	___%	___%	☐	n/a
You	___%	___%	☐	n/a
JTWROS	TOD: ___	TOD: ___	–	☐ TOD
You	___%	___%	☐	n/a

Notes (Roth start year, fees, basis)
Consider charity % slice
>5-year clock? ☐ Yes
Embedded gains? Step-up likely
Spend during life; spouse can assume

Pro tips

- Record the **earliest Roth open year** (start the 5-year clock).
- For **taxable**, note large **unrealized gains** (step-up relevance).
- Flag high-fee/legacy accounts to simplify later.

Minute 4–6 — Assign "who gets what" (tax-smart)

Use a simple matching rule: **put the best tax treatment where it's most valuable**.

- **High-income heirs:** favor **Roth** (tax-free) and **taxable** (step-up potential).
- **Lower-income heirs / charity:** can absorb more **pre-tax**; or name **charity** as a **% beneficiary** on an IRA slice.
- **Spouse:** often receives **Roth** and **taxable**; consider splitting **pre-tax** between spouse and **charity** to reduce the spouse's future RMDs.

One-line "map" (write it):
Roth → [Heir A, %]; Taxable → [Heir A/B, %]; Pre-tax → [Heir B, %] + Charity [% EIN ____].

Edge cases

- **Special-needs heir:** route via a **special-needs trust** (protect benefits).
- **Minor heirs:** use **custodian (UTMA)** or trust; avoid naming minors outright.

Minute 7–9 — Fix the paperwork
Paper beats intention. Make it match.

- **Update beneficiary forms** at each custodian: **Primary + Contingent**, percentages totaling **100%**, and **per stirpes** where desired. Ask for a **beneficiary confirmation letter**.
- Add **TOD/POD** on **taxable/bank** accounts to bypass probate (and keep step-up potential intact).
- **Align** with your **will/trust** (no conflicts). If a trust is beneficiary, have your attorney confirm **conduit vs. accumulation** language.
- Ensure at least **one Roth** has been open **>5 tax years** (open/fund now if not; even a small contribution/conversion starts the clock).
- Update your **Document Locator** (where originals live; how to access).

Minute 10–12 — Write the "10-Year Heir Play"
Give heirs a page they can actually use. Paste this into your Legacy Brief and fill the blanks.
For inherited retirement accounts (non-spouse):
• Within 30–60 days: Contact [Custodian], request "inherited IRA/Roth" titling. Provide death certificate. • 10-year rule: Account must be emptied by 12/31 of the 10th year after death. • Withdrawal pacing: Spread over years to avoid bracket spikes; coordinate with CPA. • Roth: Withdrawals tax-free if decedent's Roth was open ≥5 tax years (see Roth start year: 20__). • Traditional/Pre-tax: Taxable as ordinary income when withdrawn; consider multi-year plan.
For spouse beneficiary (options):
• You may treat as your own (rollover) or remain a beneficiary; choose with CPA based on age/RMD timing.
For taxable accounts:
• Basis step-up likely to date-of-death value (confirm with CPA/custodian). • You may hold or sell; gains measured from stepped-up basis.

Contacts block:

Role	Name	Phone	Email
CPA		(__)	
Attorney		(__)	
Advisor		(__)	
Key custodian		(__)	
Key custodian		(__)	

One-Page Worksheet (fill this now)

Section	Field	Value / Notes
ASSET MAP	Roth →	____________________ (%)
ASSET MAP	Pre-tax →	____________________ (%) + Charity ____% (EIN ______)
ASSET MAP	Taxable (TOD/POD) →	_______________ (%)
ASSET MAP	HSA → Spouse?	☐ Yes ☐ No (Spend during life plan: ____)
ASSET MAP	Roth earliest open year	20__ (≥5 tax years? ☐ Yes)
BENEFICIARIES	Primary	____________________ (%)
BENEFICIARIES	Contingent	____________________ (%)
BENEFICIARIES	Per stirpes	☐ Yes ☐ No
BENEFICIARIES	TOD/POD set	☐ Yes ☐ No
BENEFICIARIES	Confirmation letters saved	☐ Yes
LEGACY BRIEF	10-year heir play included	☐ Yes
LEGACY BRIEF	Contacts listed (CPA/Attorney/Advisor/Custodians)	☐ Yes
SHARE & REVIEW	Legacy Brief location	______________________________
SHARE & REVIEW	Told executor + backup (names)	____________________ / ____________________
SHARE & REVIEW	Annual review date (birthday month)	__ / __

Minute 13–15 — Package and share

Make it findable and durable.

- Create a **one-page Legacy Brief** with:
  - **Who gets what** (percentages), the **Roth start year**, 10-year rule summary
  - Account list, policy numbers, and **contact info**
  - "**First 30–60 days**" checklist (death certificates, inherited account setup, mail forwarding, title updates)
- Store with **will/trust/POAs** (and secure digital access instructions).

- Tell your **executor** and **one backup exactly where it lives**; add an **annual review** in your **birthday month** (and after life events).

Quick scripts (copy/paste)
Custodian — beneficiary update
Please send links/forms to update primary and contingent beneficiaries for accounts [####]. Use the following percentages and select "per stirpes" where available. Provide a confirmation letter once processed.
Attorney — coordination check
Subject: Beneficiary & TOD alignment with will/trust Hi [Name]—I've updated retirement beneficiaries and added TOD on taxable accounts. Please confirm these align with my will/trust and note any conduit/accumulation trust considerations.

"Where it lives" note to executor + backup
Subject: Legacy Brief & documents — location My Legacy Brief (with the 10-year heir play) and originals of will/trust/POAs are in [location]. Digital copies and passwords are in [vault/app], access via [instructions]. CPA/Attorney/Advisor contacts are on page 1.
Done = your beneficiaries are current, assets are mapped **tax-smart**, heirs have a plain-English **10-year plan**, and your executor knows **where to start**.

Real-World Examples (short & practical)

Numbers are **illustrative** so you can see the mechanics. Plug in your own brackets, balances, and state rules before acting.
1) High-earner kids, Roth first
Pat & Lee

- **Snapshot:** Two adult children in top tax brackets; charitable intent each year. Assets: **$600k Traditional IRA, $180k Roth IRA, $250k taxable**.
- **Design moves:**
  - **Roth IRA → Kids 50/50.** Each inherits **$90k** Roth. Under the 10-year rule, they can withdraw on their schedule; **earnings are tax-free** if Pat & Lee's Roth clock was already ≥5 tax years.
  - **Traditional IRA → 80% Kids / 20% Charity.** Charity inherits **$120k pre-tax** and pays **no income tax**. Kids split the remaining **$480k** (**$240k** each) and pace withdrawals to avoid bracket spikes.
  - **Taxable → TOD to Kids.** Likely **step-up in basis** at death; kids decide whether to hold or sell with minimal capital gains.
- **Directional tax effect:**

- The **$120k** directed to charity removes **$120k** of ordinary income the kids would have recognized.
- If the kids are ~**35%** federal bracket, that's roughly **$42k** of federal tax **avoided** (0.35 × 120,000), **plus** any state tax.

- **Paperwork:** Update IRA beneficiaries with **percentages** (incl. charity), confirm **per stirpes** for kids, set **TOD** on the brokerage, and record the **Roth start year** in the Legacy Brief.
- **Why it works:** Puts the **most-taxed** asset (pre-tax IRA) to the **non-taxed** recipient (charity), while high-earnings heirs receive **Roth/taxable** for better after-tax outcomes.

2) Blended family clarity — clean lanes
Kim

- **Snapshot:** Second marriage; wants spouse secure and adult children to receive a defined share. Assets: **$420k Traditional IRA**, **$140k Roth IRA**, **$300k taxable**.
- **Design moves:**
    - **Traditional IRA: Spouse = primary (100%), Kids = contingent (per stirpes)**. Spouse can **treat as own** or remain beneficiary and time withdrawals.
    - **Roth IRA: 50% Spouse / 50% Kids (per stirpes)** so each gets a **tax-free** bucket.
    - **Taxable:** Title **TOD to Kids** so it **skips probate** and likely gets a **basis step-up**; spouse keeps their own assets intact for liquidity.
- **Coordination checks:** Attorney verifies will/trust language aligns with **beneficiary/TOD** design; confirms any trust beneficiaries (if used) have **conduit/accumulation** terms set correctly.
- **Why it works:** Prevents accidental disinheritance, preserves step-up on taxable, and keeps the spouse's options open without mixing probate and beneficiary pathways.

3) HSA reality check — spend it during life
Omar

- **Snapshot:** Single; **$80k HSA**, **$160k Roth**, **$220k taxable**; plans to leave assets to two nieces (non-spouse heirs).
- **Issue:** A **non-spouse** inheriting an HSA generally recognizes the **entire HSA** as **taxable income** in the year of death.
- **Design moves (now):**
    - Use HSA for **qualified medical** expenses **today**: Medicare Part B/D premiums after 65, dental/vision/hearing, long-term-care premiums (within limits), and out-of-pocket costs.

    - If Omar has **prior unreimbursed** qualified expenses, he can **reimburse himself** from the HSA (with receipts).
    - Keep **Roth** and **taxable** for heirs; those are far more **heir-friendly**.
- **Directional plan:** If Omar spends **$8k/yr** from HSA on eligible costs, the $80k balance is largely **used up tax-free** over ~10 years, leaving **Roth/taxable** to the nieces.
- **Why it works:** Converts what would be a **taxable inheritance** to **tax-free spending** during Omar's life, preserving the **good assets** for heirs.

Common guardrails across all three

- Keep **beneficiary forms** current (primary **and** contingent), use **per stirpes** where intended, and get **written confirmations** from custodians.
- Record the **Roth earliest open year** so heirs know the 5-year clock is satisfied for **tax-free earnings**.
- Pair **charitable gifts** with **pre-tax IRA** dollars (at death via beneficiary %, or during life via **QCDs** if 70½+).
- Use **TOD/POD** thoughtfully on taxable/bank accounts to bypass probate **without** derailing step-up or your estate plan.
- Re-review after life events (marriage, divorce, birth/adoption, death) and **annually**.

Educational, not legal/tax advice – coordinate specifics with your CPA/attorney.

Mini Case Story — "Right asset, right heir"

Nora (68) & Sam (69)

- **Assets:** $650,000 Traditional IRA • $180,000 Roth IRA (open **8 years**) • $220,000 taxable brokerage
- **Heirs:** Alex (**high earner**) and Riley (**moderate income**)
- **Charitable intent:** Ongoing support for a local charity

Design (who gets what – and why)

1. **Roth IRA → Alex (100%)**
    - **Why:** Alex is in a top bracket; **tax-free Roth** is most valuable to a high-earner.
    - **Rule check:** Roth has been open **>5 tax years**, so **earnings are tax-free** to Alex during the 10-year window.
2. **Traditional IRA → 75% Riley / 25% Charity (direct beneficiary)**
    - **Why:**
        - Riley can pace withdrawals to fit a **moderate** bracket.

        - The **charity pays no income tax**, so the most-taxed asset goes to the **non-taxed recipient**.
    - **Directional math:**
        - Charity share: **25% × $650,000 = $162,500** (all income-tax-free to the charity).
        - Riley share: **75% × $650,000 = $487,500**. If he spreads this evenly across 10 years, that's about **$48,750/yr** of ordinary income before growth.
            - At a 22% federal rate, tax ≈ **$10,725/yr** (48,750 × 0.22 = 10,725), plus any state tax.
        - Without the charity slice, heirs would have recognized tax on the extra **$162,500** of IRA income.
3. **Taxable brokerage → TOD split 50/50 to Alex & Riley**
    - **Why:** Likely **step-up in basis** at death; each receives **$110,000** at date-of-death value. They can **hold or sell** with minimal capital gains from there.
    - **Note:** Titling as **TOD** avoids probate and keeps the estate plan clean.

Paperwork they completed

- **Beneficiary forms updated** (with **percentages**, **per stirpes** for the kids):
    - Traditional IRA: **Riley 75%**, **Local Charity 25%** (legal name & **EIN** on file)
    - Roth IRA: **Alex 100%**
- **Brokerage TOD**: 50% Alex / 50% Riley
- **Legacy Brief** created with: account list, Roth **start year**, 10-year rule explainer, custodian contacts, first-30-days checklist

The heirs' 10-year plays (what they actually do)

- **Alex (Roth beneficiary):**
    - Opens an **inherited Roth IRA** within 30–60 days (custodian assist).
    - Empties by **December 31 of the 10th year**; takes **tax-free** withdrawals as needed (Roth clock satisfied).
    - Coordinates timing with bonus/stock-comp years—even though Roth is tax-free, he might keep it growing longer and spend higher-tax assets first.
- **Riley (Traditional IRA beneficiary):**
    - Opens an **inherited IRA** within 30–60 days.
    - Targets **~$48,750/yr** (plus growth adjustments) so withdrawals **don't spike** brackets or **IRMAA** (if applicable).

    - Re-checks annually with a CPA; can front-load in **lower-income** years or slow down in **high-income** years.
    - If Riley charitably inclined, can give from **his own cash flow**; (QCDs apply to the original owner's IRA, not to inherited IRAs for most beneficiaries).
- **Both (Taxable TOD):**
    - Confirm **stepped-up basis** with the custodian.
    - Decide to hold or sell; gains measured from stepped-up value.

Directional impact

- **Tax drag reduced:** Shifting **$162,500** of pre-tax IRA to **charity** removes that income from the kids' returns entirely.
- **Bracket control:** Riley can **smooth** ~$48.8k/yr over a decade instead of facing large lump-sum income.
- **Tax-free growth preserved:** Alex inherits **$180,000** Roth with **tax-free** optionality for 10 years.
- **Friction avoided:** TOD + beneficiary designations **bypass probate**, speeding access and cutting paperwork.

Scripts they used
Custodian — beneficiary updates
"Please update beneficiaries as follows:
• Traditional IRA: **Riley 75% (per stirpes)**, **[Local Charity legal name], EIN [xx-xxxxxxx] 25%**.
• Roth IRA: **Alex 100% (per stirpes)**.
Send **written confirmations** once processed."
Brokerage — add TOD
"Add **Transfer-on-Death**: **50% Alex**, **50% Riley**. Provide confirmation and TOD registration details."
Attorney — coordination check
"We updated retirement beneficiaries and added brokerage TOD. Please confirm alignment with our will/trust and advise on any trust language (conduit vs. accumulation) we should consider."

What goes in their Legacy Brief (front page)

- **Account map:** who gets what (with %), **Roth earliest open year**, and the **10-year rule** summary
- **Contacts:** CPA, attorney, advisor, and custodian phone numbers

- **First 30–60 days:** order multiple death certificates; contact custodians to title **inherited IRA/Roth**; confirm **stepped-up basis** on taxable; update withholding/estimates as needed

Outcome (why this is the "right asset, right heir")

- **Kids avoid bracket spikes**: Riley spreads taxable IRA income; Alex keeps tax-free optionality.
- **Charity impact increases**: Pre-tax dollars go where they're **never taxed**.
- **Probate friction reduced**: Clear beneficiary/TOD titling + a one-page roadmap make administration fast and predictable.

Educational only; coordinate specifics with your CPA/attorney

Pro Tips, Scripts & Shortcuts

Use these copy-paste blocks and mini-checklists to lock in a clean, tax-smart legacy handoff.

1) Email to attorney (coordination)

Subject options (pick one):

- Beneficiary + TOD/POD coordination with will/trust
- Quick review: conduit vs. accumulation language on retirement trusts

Body (copy/paste):

Hi [Name] — I'm updating beneficiary designations and TOD/POD titles. Please confirm: 1) Beneficiary forms (primary/contingent, per stirpes) align with my will/trust. 2) Any retirement-account trusts use the right language (conduit vs. accumulation) for SECURE-era rules. 3) Titling for taxable accounts (JTWROS/community property) won't undermine basis step-up goals. 4) Whether my 401(k)/ERISA plan requires spousal consent for a non-spouse primary beneficiary. Attached: current beneficiary confirmations, proposed % map by account, and my one-page Legacy Brief. Thanks, [Your Name]

Attorney handoff checklist

- ☐ Will/trust last updated **[date]**
- ☐ List of accounts with **type** (Roth/Pre-tax/Taxable/HSA)
- ☐ Proposed **% allocations** (incl. charity EINs)
- ☐ Per stirpes preference noted
- ☐ Community-property/joint-title notes included

2) Custodian message (beneficiary update)
Secure message / email (copy/paste):
Please send links/forms to update

Account (Last 4 / Plan)	Account Type	Beneficiary Tier	Name (or Charity legal name)	SSN (last 4, if req.)	%	Per stirpes?
[Account #xxxx]	Traditional IRA	Primary			____%	☐ Yes ☐ No
[Account #xxxx]	Traditional IRA	Contingent			____%	☐ Yes ☐ No
[Account #xxxx]	Traditional IRA	**Charity** (IRA only)			____%	NA
[Account #yyyy]	Roth IRA	Primary			____%	☐ Yes ☐ No
[Account #yyyy]	Roth IRA	Contingent			____%	☐ Yes ☐ No
[Plan – 401(k)/403(b)]	Employer Plan	Primary			____%	☐ Yes ☐ No
[Plan – 401(k)/403(b)]	Employer Plan	Contingent			____%	☐ Yes ☐ No

Please confirm once processed and provide a beneficiary confirmation letter for my records.

Add TOD/POD on taxable/bank accounts

Please add Transfer-on-Death (TOD) registration as follows for account [#xxxx]:

- [Name] ____%
- [Name] ____% Send written confirmation of the new TOD registration.

Post-change sanity check (do this after confirmations arrive)

- ☐ Percentages total **100%** (primary and contingent each)
- ☐ **Per stirpes** applied where intended
- ☐ Charity listed with **legal name + EIN**
- ☐ Names/titles exactly match IDs/trust documents
- ☐ 401(k)/ERISA plan: **spousal consent** on file if needed

3) Letter to heirs (cover note)
Plain-English version (print + save as PDF):

Subject: Where to start (if something happens) Please call: • Advisor: [Name, phone, email] • CPA: [Name, phone, email] • Attorney: [Name, phone, email] Accounts: • Retirement (IRA/Roth/401k): open "inherited" accounts within 30–60 days; most must be emptied by 12/31 of the 10th year. CPA will help pace withdrawals to avoid tax spikes. • Roth IRA: tax-free to you if my Roth was open ≥5 tax years (it was opened in 20__). • Taxable brokerage: likely step-up in basis at my death—confirm basis before selling. Documents: • My Legacy Brief, will/trust/POAs, and beneficiary confirmations are at: [location / digital vault]. • Custodians to contact: [Firm + phone]. Thank you — this is meant to make everything simple. Love, [Your Name]

Executor's 30–60 day micro-checklist

- ☐ Order **multiple death certificates**
- ☐ Contact custodians; request **inherited IRA/Roth** titling
- ☐ Confirm **stepped-up basis** on taxable accounts
- ☐ Update mailing, stop autopays as needed; secure digital access

4) Quick guardrails (pin these to your Legacy Brief)

- **Charity gets pre-tax first:** Leave a **$ amount or %** of **Traditional IRA** to charity (never taxed), keep **Roth/taxable** for family.
- **Roth 5-year clock:** Ensure at least one Roth is **≥5 tax years** old; record the **earliest Roth start year**.
- **Review cadence:** After life events (marriage/divorce, birth/adoption, death, move), account changes, or annually (birthday month).
- **Don't name the estate** as beneficiary unless counsel advises (can add tax delay/complexity).
- **Minors/special needs:** Use **UTMA or trusts** (not direct); special-needs trust to protect benefits.
- **ERISA plans (401k): Spousal consent** required to name a non-spouse primary.

5) Optional add-ons (handy but fast)
"Where-it-lives" email (to executor + backup):
Subject: Legacy Brief location and access My Legacy Brief, will/trust/POAs, and beneficiary confirmations are stored at: • Physical: [Location] • Digital: [Vault/app] — access via [instructions] Contacts are on page 1 (Advisor/CPA/Attorney). Please keep this note in a safe place.

Change log (half page in your binder): example

Date	What changed	Accounts affected	New %	Notes/Confirm ID
20__// Added charity 10% on IRA Vanguard IRA			10% Conf #____	

5-minute annual audit

- ☐ Beneficiary confirmations match **intent**
- ☐ TOD/POD still correct
- ☐ Roth **start year** recorded; still ≥5
- ☐ Legacy Brief updated; contacts current
- ☐ Heirs/executor reminded where it lives

These small scripts and guardrails keep the legal/tax plumbing aligned so your plan is simple for loved ones and ruthless on unnecessary taxes.

Tools & Printables You'll Use

1) Beneficiary Map (one page)

Purpose: a snapshot of "who gets what," by **tax type**, with proof-ready details.

BENEFICIARY MAP — One Page

Owner	**Date**	**Version**
____________________	____ / ____ / _____	v____

Account / Custodian	Type (Roth / Pre-tax / Taxable / HSA)	Primary Beneficiary(ies) %	Contingent %	Per stirpes?	EIN (if charity)
____________________	__________	____%	____%	☐ Yes ☐ No	__________
____________________	__________	____%	____%	☐ Yes ☐ No	__________
____________________	__________	____%	____%	☐ Yes ☐ No	__________

Notes (Roth start yr, TOD/POD, trust) ____

____

Account / Custodian	Type	Primary Beneficiary(ies) %	Contingent %	Per stirpes?	EIN (if charity)	Notes
Vanguard IRA #1234	Pre-tax	Riley 75%; City Food Bank 25%	Kids equally	☐ Yes ☐ No	12-3456789	Charity on pre-tax; per stirpes for kids
Fidelity Roth #9876	Roth (opened 2017)	Alex 100%	Riley 100%	☐ Yes ☐ No	–	5-yr clock met (2017)
Schwab Taxable #5555	Taxable (TOD)	TOD: Alex 50%; Riley 50%	–	–	–	Step-up likely; confirm at death
Bank HSA #4444	HSA	Spouse 100%	–	–	–	Spend during life; spouse may assume

How to use: Print, sign, and store with **beneficiary confirmations** from each custodian. Update **version** each time you change anything.

2) Legacy Brief (for heirs/executor)
Purpose: a plain-English road map to avoid delays, probate confusion, and tax mistakes.
Contacts
LEGACY BRIEF — For Heirs & Executor (1–2 pages)
Where to start (first 7 days):

Role	Name	Phone	Email
Advisor	________	(__) -	________________
CPA	________	(__) -	________________
Attorney	________	(__) -	________________

Immediate Tasks

Task	Details / Status
Order death certificates	Order __ copies
Mail forwarding	Set up with USPS
Secure home & digital logins	________________________________

Key Accounts (High Level)

Account	Custodian	Phone	Beneficiaries / Notes
IRA (Pre-tax)	______	______	Beneficiaries: ______ / ______
Roth IRA (Opened: 20__)	______	______	Beneficiaries: ______
Brokerage (Taxable, TOD on file)	______	______	–
HSA	______	______	Spouse may assume; non-spouse: taxable
Life Insurance / Annuities	______	______	Policy # ______; Carrier ______

10-Year Rule (Retirement Accounts)

Heir type	Required action	Deadline / Timing
Non-spouse heirs	Open inherited IRA/Roth	Within 30–60 days
Non-spouse heirs	Empty by 12/31 of the 10th year	12/31 in year 10
Spouse	May roll over or remain beneficiary (CPA/attorney to advise)	–

Step-Up in Basis (Taxable Accounts)

Asset type	Action	Notes
Brokerage / Taxable assets	Check for basis step-up at death before selling	Confirm cost basis with custodian prior to any sale

Documents & Access

Item	Location / App	Access Steps
Physical originals	____________________	____________________
Digital vault / app	____________________	____________________

My Wishes

Field	Details
Charities I support	
Family contact tree	

3) 10-Year Heir Play Card

Purpose: a wallet-sized set of rules heirs can follow without reading the tax code.

10-YEAR HEIR PLAY CARD — Retirement Accounts

1) Title correctly (within 30–60 days)

• Call custodian to open "Inherited IRA" or "Inherited Roth IRA." Provide death certificate.

2) Know your clock

• Non-spouse: Account must be emptied by 12/31 of the 10th year after death.

• Spouse: Options available (own vs. beneficiary).

Ask CPA which fits your age & RMD timing.

3) Pace withdrawals (avoid spikes)

• Coordinate with CPA to spread withdrawals across years that keep you below tax and IRMAA cliffs.
• Roth: tax-free if decedent's Roth was open ≥5 tax years (Roth start year: 20__).
4) Keep proof
• Save all custodian confirmations and year-end 1099-R forms. Track remaining balance vs. the 10-year deadline.

4) Charitable Plan Sheet
Purpose: decide **now** whether charity receives part of **pre-tax** at death, or you'll use **QCDs** during life.
CHARITABLE PLAN

Item	**Value / Notes**
Annual QCD target ($)	__________
From IRA custodian	__________
Charity / EIN	____________________
Acknowledgment letters saved?	☐ Yes
Where stored	__________________________
Traditional IRA charity % (at death)	______%
Charity legal name (at death)	____________________
Charity EIN (at death)	______________
Rationale	Direct pre-tax to non-taxed recipient; family receives Roth/taxable.

Notes:(DAF/private foundation restrictions, multi-charity splits, successor advisors):
____

5) Document Locator

Purpose: show **exactly** where originals and digital credentials live.

Item	Value / Notes
Document Locator (Will / Trust / POAs)	
Beneficiary Confirmations	
Life Insurance & Annuities	
Property Titles / Deeds	
Tax Returns (Last 3 Years)	
Digital Vault / Password Manager	
Access (Vault/Password Manager)	
Safe Deposit Box – Bank	
Safe Deposit Box – Box #	
Safe Deposit Box – Key Location	
Contacts (Advisor / CPA / Attorney)	On Legacy Brief pt.1

6) Annual Review Checklist
Purpose: a 5-minute audit that keeps everything current.

ANNUAL REVIEW (Birthday Month) — 5-Minute Audit Life changes?
☐ Marriage/divorce
☐ Birth/adoption
☐ Death
☐ Move (state)
☐ New charity or % change Beneficiaries & titles
☐ Primary & Contingent still correct (total 100%)
☐ Per stirpes set where intended
☐ TOD/POD on taxable/bank correct
☐ 401(k) spousal consent (if non-spouse beneficiary) Roth & HSA specifics
☐ Roth earliest open year: 20__ (≥5 tax years? ☐ Yes)
☐ Add note if not yet met
☐ HSA: spend-down plan active (premiums/medical)
☐ Spouse knows HSA rules Charitable plan
☐ QCD amount this year (70½+): $_______
☐ Charity EINs verified
☐ Acknowledgments filed
☐ IRA % to charity at death still right: ______% Binder & access
☐ Legacy Brief updated (v____)
☐ Document Locator current
☐ Executor & backup reminded where it lives
Next review date: ____ / ____ / ______

Print-Ready Bundle (how to package)

- **Front tab:** *Legacy Brief* (v# and date stamped).
- **Tab 1:** *Beneficiary Map* + **beneficiary confirmations** (PDF printouts).
- **Tab 2:** *10-Year Heir Play Card* (shrink to half-page; place 2 copies).
- **Tab 3:** *Charitable Plan Sheet* (with charity **EINs**).
- **Tab 4:** *Document Locator* (plus copies of will/trust/POAs if allowed).
- **Back pocket:** Most recent **account statements** and **tax return summary** (Form 1040 pg.1–2).

Versioning tip: File-name convention: LegacyBrief_[YourLastName]_v03_2025-08-17.pdf (update the **v#** and **date** every time you change anything).

Security tip: Keep one **printed binder** in your home safe + one **encrypted PDF** in a password manager/digital vault. Share **location and access** with your executor and one backup.

Action Step (what to complete now)

Objective: leave this pillar with a **tax-smart inheritance map** and a printable **Legacy Brief** your heirs/executor can follow in minutes.

1) Update beneficiaries (do this first)

- **Accounts list:** IRA(s), Roth IRA(s), 401(k)/403(b), HSA, annuities, life insurance.
- **Set/confirm for each:**
  - **Primary + Contingent** percentages = **100%** each layer
  - **Per stirpes** where desired
  - **Charity** entries show **legal name + EIN**
  - (ERISA plans) **Spousal consent** on file if naming a non-spouse primary
- **Ask for: Beneficiary confirmation letters** from each custodian. File them behind your Beneficiary Map.
- **Optional:** Add **TOD/POD** on taxable/bank accounts to bypass probate (keep step-up potential intact).

2) Map assets to heirs (tax-smart placement)

- **Rule of thumb:**
  - **Roth → higher earners** (most valuable tax-free)
  - **Pre-tax → lower earners/charity** (least tax drag)
  - **Taxable → either** (likely step-up in basis)
- **Write your map (sample):**

Roth → [Heir A __%] Pre-tax IRA → [Heir B __%] + [Charity __% (EIN ________)]
Taxable (TOD) → [Heir A __%] / [Heir B __%]

- **Edge cases:** minors → UTMA/trust; special-needs → special-needs trust (attorney review).

3) Check the Roth clock

- **Record earliest Roth open year:** 20__
- **If < 5 tax years:** start the clock now (small **contribution** or **conversion**) and note the year in your Legacy Brief.
- **Add this line to the Brief: "Roth opened in 20__** (≥5-year clock for tax-free earnings)."

4) Write the Legacy Brief (1–2 pages)

Include:

- **Contacts:** Advisor, CPA, Attorney + phone/email
- **Account list:** custodian names, last-4, who inherits what (with %), **Roth start year**
- **"First 30–60 days" steps:** order death certificates; open **inherited IRA/Roth**; confirm **step-up** on taxable; mail/auto-pay cleanup
- **10-Year rule** summary for non-spouse heirs; spouse options in one line
- **Document access:** where originals live; digital vault/password manager instructions
- **Charity section:** QCD plan (if 70½+) and any IRA % to charity (legal name + EIN)

5) Set the charitable slice

- **During life (70½+):** QCD target $________ from **IRA → charity (direct)** each year; keep acknowledgment letters.
- **At death:** assign __% of **Traditional IRA** to **[Charity, EIN]** on the beneficiary form.
- **Email your custodian (template):**

Please add [Charity legal name], EIN [xx-xxxxxxx], as __% beneficiary on my Traditional IRA #____. Send a beneficiary confirmation letter once processed.

6) Tell your executor (and one backup) + schedule annual review

- **"Where it lives" note (send today):** location of the **Legacy Brief**, will/trust/POAs, beneficiary confirmations, and digital access.
- **Calendar:** set an **annual review** in your **birthday month** (and after any life event).

One-Page Worksheet (fill now)

Beneficiaries updated? ☐ Yes (Confirm letters filed: ☐)

Per stirpes applied where intended? ☐ Yes

ASSET MAP Roth → ____________________ %

Pre-tax IRA → ____________________ % + Charity ____% (EIN ___________)

Taxable (TOD/POD) → ____________________ %

HSA plan (spouse or spend-down): ____

Roth earliest open year: 20__ (≥5 tax years? ☐ Yes ☐ No → start clock)

LEGACY BRIEF

Contacts listed (Advisor/CPA/Attorney)?

☐ 10-Year rule & spouse options summarized?

☐ Document access (physical + digital) noted?

☐ CHARITABLE PLAN QCD (70½+): $________ / yr

Custodian set?

☐ IRA % to charity at death: ____% (EIN ___________)

Form updated?

☐ SHARE & REVIEW Executor told location?

☐ Backup told? ☐ Annual review date (MM/DD): ____ / ____

Micro-scripts (copy/paste)

Custodian (beneficiaries/TOD)

Please update PRIMARY and CONTINGENT beneficiaries for account [#____] per the attached percentages (per stirpes where available). For taxable account [#____], add TOD as follows: [Name __%], [Name __%]. Email written confirmations when complete.

Attorney (coordination)

Confirm beneficiary/TOD updates align with my will/trust. Flag any conduit vs. accumulation trust language to adjust for SECURE-era rules.

Executor note (where it lives)

My Legacy Brief and originals are at [location]. Digital copies in [vault/app], access via [instructions]. Call Advisor/CPA/Attorney listed on page 1.

Deliverable

A **tax-smart inheritance map + Legacy Brief** that keeps transfers **fast**, avoids avoidable **taxes**, and gives heirs a **clear 10-year plan**. *(Educational only – coordinate specifics with your attorney/CPA.)*

Pillar 5 — Executive Summary (Tax-Free Legacy Planning)

Introduction & Key Points

- **Aim:** Get the *right assets to the right heirs* with minimal tax, zero confusion, and no probate delays.
- **Core idea:** Favor **Roth** for high-tax heirs, **pre-tax** for lower-tax heirs or **charity**, and let **taxable** benefit from a potential **step-up in basis**. Clean **beneficiary forms** do the heavy lifting.

The Rationale (plain English)

- **Buckets behave differently:**
  - **Roth:** heirs generally must empty in 10 years, but withdrawals are tax-free if the owner's **5-year clock** is met.
  - **Pre-tax:** creates **taxable income** for heirs—often in peak earning years.
  - **Taxable:** may get a **basis step-up** at death.
- **Design > default:** Up-to-date beneficiary forms avoid probate and control who gets what.
- **Charitable carve-outs:** Direct **IRA % to charity** or use **QCDs (70½+)**; send the most-taxed asset to the non-taxed recipient.
- **Simplicity:** A plain-English **Legacy Brief** saves months of confusion.

Key Mechanics (what trips people up)

- **Beneficiary forms rule** retirement accounts (they can trump the will). Use **primary + contingent** and **per stirpes** as desired.
- **SECURE-era 10-year rule** for most non-spouse heirs; spouses have flexible options (own/rollover/beneficiary). Trusts need conduit vs. accumulation language.
- **Roth details:** no lifetime RMDs; heirs get 10 years; ensure **5-year clock** satisfied.
- **HSA:** great for you; bad to leave to non-spouse (generally taxable to them).
- **Taxable & titling:** step-up potential; consider **TOD/POD**; local titling rules matter.
- **Coordination risk:** misalignment between will/trust and beneficiary/TOD creates surprises—review after life events.

Readiness Quiz (score quickly)

- 7 yes/no checks on: current beneficiaries, tax-smart asset map, 10-year understanding, Roth clock, QCD/charity plan, Legacy Brief on file, and whether key people know where documents live.

- **0–2:** beneficiaries + Brief • **3–5:** map assets + Roth/QCD plan • **6–7:** finalize and calendar annual review.

Step-by-Step Implementation (10–15 minutes)

1. **Inventory & label** each account (Roth/Pre-tax/Taxable/HSA).
2. **Assign who gets what** (Roth → high earners; Pre-tax → lower earners/charity; Taxable → either).
3. **Fix paperwork** (beneficiaries, per stirpes, TOD/POD; ensure a Roth >5 years old).
4. **Write the 10-Year Heir Play** (inherited account setup, pacing withdrawals, contacts).
5. **Package & share** a one-page **Legacy Brief**; tell executor and a backup where it lives; set an annual review.

Real-World Examples (short & practical)

- **Roth to high-tax kids + IRA % to charity:** reduces heirs' taxable income and boosts impact.
- **Blended family clarity:** spouse primary, kids contingent (per stirpes), taxable as TOD to kids.
- **HSA spend-down:** use for your medical/Medicare now; leave Roth/taxable to heirs.

Mini Case Story — "Right asset, right heir"

- **Nora & Sam:** Roth → high-earner child; Traditional IRA **75%** → moderate-income child and **25%** → charity; Taxable → TOD 50/50. Outcome: fewer bracket spikes, higher charitable efficiency, faster administration.

Pro Tips, Scripts & Shortcuts

- **Attorney email:** confirm beneficiary/TOD alignment with will/trust; trust language.
- **Custodian messages:** update beneficiaries (percentages, per stirpes), add TOD/POD, request confirmations.
- **Heir cover note:** who to call, 30–60 day steps, 10-year rule, Roth clock, document location.
- **Guardrails:** charity gets **pre-tax** first; record **Roth start year**; review annually/after life events.

Tools & Printables You'll Use

- **Beneficiary Map (one page) • Legacy Brief • 10-Year Heir Play Card • Charitable Plan Sheet (QCD/IRA %)**
  • Document Locator • Annual Review Checklist.

Action Step (what to complete now)

- Update beneficiaries (primary/contingent, per stirpes; add TOD/POD).
- Map assets to heirs by tax character; verify **Roth ≥5 years**.
- Draft the **Legacy Brief** (contacts, accounts, first-month steps).
- Set the **charity slice** (QCD now and/or IRA % at death).
- Tell your **executor + backup** where the packet lives; schedule an **annual review**.

Educational only – coordinate final decisions with your attorney/CPA.

Pillar 6 — The 15-Minute Tax-Free Action Plan

Introduction and Key Points

This is the capstone. In the next 15 minutes you'll turn everything from Pillars 1–5 into a **dated, dollar-specific game plan** you can execute without second-guessing. No theory—just the exact moves to lock in **lower lifetime taxes**, **IRMAA safety**, and **clean inheritance mechanics**.

Quick win (what you'll walk away with):

- A **this-year Roth conversion amount** (with a built-in buffer) and target **execution window**.
- Your **RMD/QCD cadence** and **withholding** settings so taxes are on rails.
- A **3–5 year conversion ladder** sized to your bracket and IRMAA tiers.
- A **market-dip trigger** ("If −%, **convert up to $** within buffers").
- **Beneficiary/TOD** confirmations + a one-page **Legacy Brief** location note.
- Two copy-paste emails: **CPA check** and **custodian instructions**—ready to send.
- Three calendar holds: **Mid-Year Review**, **Nov/Dec True-Up**, and an **Annual Legacy check**.

What you need on your desk (2 minutes):

- Last year's **Form 1040**, year-to-date income, and your target **top bracket** (22%/24%).
- Your **IRMAA tier** reference and current **headroom** from Pillar 1/3.
- Account list: **pre-tax / Roth / taxable / HSA** with rough balances.
- Beneficiary/TOD status (or confirmations) and charity **EINs** if relevant.

Ground rules (so you don't stall):

- **Good enough beats perfect.** Use **$2k–$5k** buffers under bracket tops and **$1k–$5k** under the next IRMAA tier.
- **Sequence matters:** RMD → QCD (if 70½+) → then any **conversion**.
- **Pay tax from cash** on conversions (0% withholding) so every dollar lands in Roth.
- **Document once, reuse forever:** Save confirmations and keep your binder/Brief current.

In the pages that follow, you'll check boxes, fill blanks, and set dates. When the timer dings, you'll have a **printable one-page Action Sheet** and scheduled touchpoints that keep you on track all year—simple, fast, and tax-smart.
(Educational only – coordinate specifics with your CPA/attorney.)

Key Points

- **Simplicity is the Goal:**
  - You don't need a complex spreadsheet or a 50-page binder to take action.
  - A focused, one-page plan ensures you actually start and stick with your tax-free strategy.
- **Three-Part Structure:**
  - **Assessment:** Review your current retirement accounts, tax situation, and beneficiary designations.
  - **Action:** Identify 1–3 immediate moves (e.g., start a Roth conversion, update beneficiaries, calculate RMD reductions).
  - **Automation:** Set recurring calendar reminders for key tasks (annual conversions, income reviews, account check-ups).
- **Permanent Low-Tax Environment:**
  - Thanks to the **2025 One Big Beautiful Bill Act**, there's no looming 2026 tax cliff—but waiting still costs you lost years of tax-free growth.
  - The earlier you start, the more compounding works in your favor.
- **Leverage Professional Support Wisely:**
  - You don't need to hire a full-time planner; use a tax pro or advisor for targeted tasks like bracket analysis or conversion execution.
- **Keep it Flexible:**
  - Life changes (retirement date, market shifts, healthcare costs) mean your plan should be reviewed annually.

Why This Matters for Retirees

- **Eliminates Procrastination:** The plan removes guesswork so you can take your first step today.
- **Builds Confidence:** Having a written roadmap ensures you know exactly what to do and when.
- **Protects More Wealth:** Every year you delay means more money potentially taxed later.
- **Creates Momentum:** Small wins in year one lead to bigger, compounding benefits in future years.

Action Step

Fill out your **One-Page Tax-Free Retirement Blueprint**:

1. **Write down your starting point:** Current account balances, tax bracket, RMD age, and beneficiary status.
2. **List your Year 1 moves:** Amount to convert, accounts to update, and any charitable/QCD plans.
3. **Set your Year 2–5 plan:** Include conversion targets, planned deductions, and review dates.
4. **Schedule reminders:** Put annual "Tax-Free Strategy Review" dates on your calendar.
5. **Commit to your first step today:** Whether it's booking a call with your advisor, starting a partial conversion, or updating a beneficiary form—do it before the day ends.

The Rationale (plain English)

Action beats analysis because taxes are a moving target and procrastination is expensive. Pillars 1–5 gave you the *ideas*; Pillar 6 turns them into a *repeatable routine* so you actually capture the savings.

Why this works (behavior, not just math)

- **Cuts decision fatigue:** One **single page** holds your bracket target, IRMAA buffer, this-year conversion, RMD/QCD plan, and contacts. Fewer moving parts → fewer stalls.
- **Pre-commits the sequence:** Checklists prevent costly misfires: **RMD → QCD (if 70½+) → conversion**; **0% withholding on conversions**; use **RMD withholding** to meet safe harbor.
- **Buffers > precision:** Taxes, markets, and distributions shift. Keeping **$2k–$5k under the bracket** and **$1k–$5k under IRMAA** absorbs surprises without paralysis.
- **Calendar → cadence:** Three holds (Mid-Year, Nov/Dec True-Up, Annual Legacy Check) create a built-in loop to **measure, adjust, and finish** before 12/31.
- **Tiny tasks, big compounding:** A few bracket-fill conversions now shrink future RMDs for years; QCDs reduce MAGI and protect IRMAA; clean beneficiaries avoid probate detours.

What the "single page + 3 emails + 3 holds" actually covers

- **Single page:** Your **Action Sheet** with: top-of-bracket, projected taxable, **planned conversion**, IRMAA buffer, RMD/QCD cadence + withholding, market-dip trigger, beneficiary/TOD check, and key contacts.
- **Three emails/messages:**
  1. **CPA true-up:** "Here are my numbers—confirm bracket/IRMAA safety and safe-harbor."
  2. **Custodian (conversion):** "Convert $___ in-kind, **0% withholding**; confirm in writing."
  3. **Custodian (RMD/QCD):** "Set **monthly/quarterly** RMD with % **withholding; process **QCD $_**** direct to [Charity, EIN]."
- **Three calendar holds:**
  - **Mid-Year (May/June):** Update income; adjust conversion/RMD withholding; recheck IRMAA headroom.
  - **Nov/Dec True-Up:** Confirm remaining **safe headroom**; optional top-off conversion before 12/31.
  - **Annual Legacy Check (birthday month):** Verify beneficiaries/TOD, Roth 5-year clock noted, Legacy Brief location shared.

Built-in guardrails (so you don't overthink)

- **Headroom math, not perfection:** Planned conversion = **(Bracket top − Projected taxable) − $2–$5k** buffer.
- **IRMAA awareness:** Keep **$1–$5k** under the next tier; remember the **two-year lookback**.
- **Market-dip trigger:** "If portfolio −%, **convert up to $_** (still inside buffers)." You act when it's advantageous—no guesswork.

The payoff

- You replace annual tax anxiety with a **15-minute routine**: numbers → instructions → dates.
- You avoid bracket creep and IRMAA surprises, keep conversions clean, and leave heirs a clear map.
- Most importantly, you **finish**—on time, under thresholds, with documentation in your binder.

Readiness Snapshot (60-second check)

How to use: Read each item. If true **today**, give yourself **1 point**. Total your score.

1) I know my target top bracket (22%/24%) and IRMAA buffer for this year.

- **How to check (30 sec):**
  - Write your target bracket (22% or 24%) and its **top-of-bracket dollar** for your filing status.
  - Note your **IRMAA tier** and keep a **$1k–$5k** cushion under the next tier (remember: **2-year lookback** on MAGI).
- **Say "Yes" if:** You can state:
  "**Target bracket:** __% (top $**). IRMAA buffer left:** $ (≥ $1k–$5k)."
- **If No (quick fix):** Grab last year's 1040 + YTD income; ask your CPA for this year's **top-of-bracket** and your **IRMAA headroom**.

2) I can name my max safe conversion (headroom minus $2k–$5k buffer).

- **How to check (20 sec):**
  - **Headroom =** (Target **top-of-bracket**) − (**Projected taxable income**).
  - **Planned conversion =** Headroom − **$2k–$5k buffer**.
- **Mini-math (illustrative):** If top-of-bracket is **$201,000** and projected taxable is **$164,500**,
  headroom = **$36,500**; planned conversion = **$31,500–$34,500** (after buffer).
- **Say "Yes" if:** You can write one number: "**Planned conversion: $_____** (buffered)."
- **If No (quick fix):** Estimate YTD income, add expected items (dividends, cap gains, RMD if any), then compute headroom and subtract your buffer.

3) My RMD status is clear (Not started / Starts in ____ / In progress with cadence).

- **How to check (10 sec):**
  - Circle one: **Not started** | **Starts in 20__** | **In progress**.
  - If in progress, note **cadence** (Monthly/Quarterly) and **withholding** (Fed __% / State __%).
- **Say "Yes" if:** You can state the status and, if applicable, your **RMD amount, cadence, and withholding**.
- **If No (quick fix):** Call custodian to confirm your first RMD year and set (or verify) an **automatic cadence** with withholding.

Score & Next Move

- **2–3 points:** You're ready to **set amounts and dates now** (proceed to the 15-Minute Plan).
- **0–1 point:** Spend 5 minutes to nail the bracket top, IRMAA buffer, and a draft conversion number—then proceed.

One-Line Worksheet (fill now)

Item	Value / Notes
Target bracket (%)	__%
Top-of-bracket ($)	________
Projected taxable ($)	________
Headroom ($)	________
Planned conversion ($) *(−$2k–$5k buffer)*	________
IRMAA buffer after conversion ($) *(≥ $1k–$5k?)*	________
RMD status	☐ Not started ☐ Starts in 20__ ☐ In progress
If RMD in progress — Cadence	☐ M ☐ Q
Withholding	Fed __% / State __%

The 15-Minute Plan (minute-by-minute)

Keep this page in front of you. Pencil in rough numbers first; perfection later. Use $2k–$5k under your bracket top and $1k–$5k under the next IRMAA tier as buffers.

Minute 0–3 — Pull the numbers

Goal: size your *safe* conversion for this year.

- **Top-of-bracket:** $________
  Tip: Use your filing status and chosen lane (22% or 24%).
- **Projected taxable income:** $________
  Include: wages/consulting, pensions, interest/dividends, capital gains, IRA/401(k) withdrawals/RMDs, rental net, taxable Social Security portion.
- **Headroom (top − projected):** $________
- **Planned conversion (headroom − $2k–$5k buffer):** $________
  Why buffer: absorbs fund distributions, surprise bonuses, or extra interest.
- **IRMAA buffer left *after* conversion:** $________
  Keep: $1k–$5k cushion under the next IRMAA tier (2-year lookback).

Mini-math (illustrative):

Top-of-22% = $201,000; projected taxable = $166,500 → headroom = $34,500.
Planned conversion = $30,000–$32,500 (leaving a ~$2k–$4.5k buffer).
IRMAA check: MAGI stays ~$2,300 under next tier → *green light.*

Minute 4–6 — Decide execution details

Goal: choose the account, how you'll move assets, and when you'll act.

- **Convert from:** ☐ IRA ☐ 401(k)/403(b) *(in-plan Roth if offered)*
  Note: If you have after-tax **basis** in IRAs, confirm Form 8606 and consider isolating basis via roll-in to an active 401(k) (if allowed) before converting.

- **Method: ☐ In-kind (preferred)** ☐ Cash
  Why in-kind: stays invested; avoids market timing.
- **Tax on conversion:** ☐ **0% withholding**; pay the tax from **cash**
  Why: keeps **100%** of the conversion landing in Roth.
- **Market-dip trigger:**
  "If portfolio **−__%** from recent high, convert **up to $______** (remaining headroom), staying under bracket/IRMAA buffers."
  Common triggers: −10% or −15%.

Pick an execution window: Dates: __ /___ /20___ **to** ___ /___ /20___ (e.g., after Q2 estimates, before year-end distributions).

Minute 7–9 — RMD/QCD & withholding on rails

Goal: make required income predictable and penalty-proof.

- **RMD this year?** ☐ No ☐ Yes → **Amount:** $_________
  Sequence: **Take RMD first**; only amounts above that can be converted.
- **Cadence:** ☐ **Monthly** ☐ **Quarterly Start:** __
  Why cadence: smooth cash flow and withholdings; easier safe-harbor compliance.
- **Withholding:** Fed __% | State __%
  Target: meet **safe harbor** (100% of last year's total tax, or 110% if prior-year AGI > $150k), or 90% of current-year.
- **QCD (age 70½+):** $________ **IRA** → **Charity** (EIN ___________),
- **target month:** ______
  Why: counts toward IRA RMD **without raising MAGI**, helping IRMAA.

Quick check: If using QCDs, do them **early**; they satisfy the *first* IRA dollars.

Minute 10–12 — Legacy & paperwork quick pass

Goal: keep inheritance mechanics clean and tax-smart.

- **Beneficiaries/TOD:** ☐ **Verified** ☐ **Update sent**
  Primary + contingent total 100%; per stirpes where desired; charities listed with legal name + EIN; TOD/POD on taxable/bank as needed.
- **Roth clock:** Earliest Roth open year: **20__** (≥5 tax years? ☐ **Yes**)
  If not, start the clock with a small contribution/conversion; note the year.
- **Legacy Brief:** ☐ **Updated**; **location** noted for executor
  Include: 10-year heir play, contacts (CPA/attorney/advisor), custodian numbers, first-30-days checklist.

Minute 13–15 — Lock it in (send + schedule)
Goal: push the plan into motion and make it automatic.

- **Email CPA** *(true-up & safe-harbor check)*
  - Confirm your planned conversion, IRMAA margin, RMD cadence, QCD amount/timing, and withholding adequacy.
- **Message custodian/plan** *(execution)*
  - **Conversion:** in-kind, $______, **0% withholding**, written confirmation.
  - **RMD cadence:** $______/yr paid ☐ M ☐ Q with Fed __% / State % **withholding; start //**.
  - **QCD:** $______ to **[Charity legal name, EIN]**, instructions + confirmation.
- **Add 3 calendar holds:**

1. **Mid-Year Review (May/June):** update income; adjust remaining headroom, withholding, QCD/RMD pace.
2. **Nov/Dec True-Up:** CPA confirms remaining safe headroom; optional small top-off conversion before **12/31**.

Annual Legacy Check (birthday month): beneficiaries/TOD, Roth clock, Legacy Brief updates.

Done = a dated, dollar-specific plan you can execute confidently—**bracket-safe, IRMAA-aware,** and legacy-ready.

One-Page Fill-In (tear-off) Year & Bracket

Item	Value / Notes
Year	______
Bracket (Top-of-bracket $)	% (Top-of-bracket $______)
Projected taxable ($)	________
Headroom ($)	________
Planned conversion ($)	________ *(buffered by $______)*
IRMAA buffer after ($)	________

Conversion

Item	Value / Notes
From	☐ IRA ☐ 401k/403b
In-kind?	☐ Yes ☐ No
Withholding	0%
Window	__ /___/20___ - __ /___/20___
Market dip trigger	−% → up to $______

RMD / QCD / Withholding

Item	Value / Notes
RMD	☐ N/A ☐ $________
Cadence	☐ M ☐ Q
Start (date)	__ /___/20___
Withholding	Fed __% / State __%
Safe harbor	☐ Met ☐ Plan __ /___/20___
QCD (age 70½+)	$________ to [Charity, EIN __________] in ______

Legacy Quick Check

Item	Value / Notes
Beneficiaries / TOD	☐ Verified ☐ Update sent
Roth start year	20__ (≥5? ☐ Yes)
Legacy Brief updated	☐ Yes
Location	______________________

Send + Schedule

Item	Value / Notes
CPA email sent	☐
Custodian messages sent	☐
Holds	Mid-Year __ /___/20___ • True-Up __ /___/20___ • Legacy Check __ /___/20___

Two-Page Action Sheet (fill now; print)

Print this on a single page and place it on top of your binder. Version/date it every time you change anything.

Action Sheet Header

Item	Value / Notes
Year ______	
Version v___	
Date ____ / ____ / ______	

Bracket Plan

Item	Value / Notes
Target bracket (%)	__%
Top-of-bracket ($)	________
Projected taxable income (YTD + expected) ($)	________
Headroom (top − projected) ($)	________
Planned Roth conversion ($)	________ *(headroom − $2k–$5k buffer)*
IRMAA buffer AFTER conversion ($)	________ *(keep $1k–$5k under next tier)*
IRMAA next tier ($)	________
Two-year lookback reminder	Noted

Conversion

Item	Value / Notes
From account	__________________ *(☐ IRA ☐ 401k/403b in-plan Roth)*
Method	☐ In-kind *(preferred)* ☐ Cash
Withholding on conversion	**0%** *(tax paid from cash outside retirement)*
Execution window	__ /___ /20___ → __ /___ /20___
Market-dip trigger	"If portfolio −**% from recent high, convert up to $**______ (remain under buffers)."
Basis check (IRAs)	Form 8606 on file? ☐ Yes ☐ No
Isolate basis plan	☐ N/A ☐ Roll-in to 401k then convert

RMD / QCD / Withholding

Item	Value / Notes
RMD this year	☐ N/A ☐ $________
Cadence	☐ Monthly ☐ Quarterly
Start (date)	__ /___ /20___
Withholding on RMD	Fed __%
Safe harbor	☐ Met ☐ Plan to adjust by __ /___ /20___
QCD (70½+, IRA only)	$________ to [Charity legal name, EIN __________] in ______ *(month)*

Item	Value / Notes
QCD acknowledgment letter saved?	☐ Yes ☐ Pending

Legacy Quick Check

Item	Value / Notes
Beneficiaries / TOD	☐ Verified ☐ Update sent *(primary + contingent total 100%; per stirpes noted)*
Roth clock	Earliest Roth open year: 20__ • ≥5 tax years? ☐ Yes ☐ No *(start clock now)*
Legacy Brief updated?	☐ Yes
Location for executor	________________________________

Notes

Item	Details
Notes (fund distributions, bonuses, property sales, medical timing, state move, etc.)	

Contacts

Item	Value / Notes
CPA	___________________________ (__) - • Email: ____________________________
Advisor	________________________ (__) - • Email: ____________________________
Custodians / Plan	_____________________________________ • Phone: ______________________
Charity contact (for QCD)	_____________________________ • Email/Phone: ________________

Sign-Off

Item	Value / Notes
CPA green-light received	☐ on __ /___ /**20**___
Custodian confirmations filed	☐ *(conversion / RMD / QCD)*

Mini "Math Key" (margin)

- **Headroom** = Top-of-bracket − Projected taxable
- **Planned conversion** = Headroom − $2k–$5k buffer
- Keep **$1k–$5k** under IRMAA tier (two-year lookback)

Optional filled example (illustrative)

Year & Version

Item	Value
Year	2025
Version	v01
Date	08/17/2025

Bracket Plan

Item	Value
Top-of-22%	$201,000
Projected taxable	$167,800
Headroom	$33,200
Planned conversion	$30,500 *(buffer ≈ $2,700)*
IRMAA buffer after	≈ $2,100

Conversion

Item	Value
Convert from	Vanguard IRA
Method	In-kind
Withholding	0%
Window	09/10–09/20
Market-dip trigger	−12% → up to +$6,000 *(stay under buffers)*

RMD / QCD

Item	Value
RMD	N/A
QCD	N/A

Legacy Quick Check

Item	Value
Beneficiaries verified	08/10/2025
Roth start year	2017
Legacy Brief location	Home safe & vault

Contacts

Role	Details
CPA	Jane Smith — (555) 123-4567
Custodian	Vanguard — (800) 662-7447

Copy-Paste Scripts (ready to send)
Email to CPA — bracket/IRMAA/safe-harbor true-up
Subject: This-year Roth conversion & RMD/QCD true-up
Hi [Name] — Please confirm these 2025 numbers and guardrails:
• Top-of-bracket $____; projected taxable $____ → headroom $____; planned conversion $____ with ~$[2–5]k buffer.
• IRMAA-safe after this move by ~$____ (next tier at $____; two-year lookback noted).
• RMD this year $____ on [Monthly/Quarterly] cadence; withholding Fed __% / State __% — does this meet safe harbor?
• QCD (if 70½+): $____ to [Charity legal name, EIN], timing [month].
• Any state-tax considerations or mutual-fund distribution timing we should watch?
If clear, I'll execute by [date]. Attachments: Action Sheet, last 1040, YTD income snapshot. Thanks!

Variation (with IRA basis):
Also, do you show any IRA basis on Form 8606? If yes, should I isolate basis by rolling pre-tax to my 401(k) (plan accepts roll-ins) before converting?
Custodian/Plan — execute conversion (secure message or call)
Please convert $[amount] from my Traditional [IRA / 401(k)/403(b)] to [Roth IRA / in-plan Roth] IN-KIND with 0% withholding.
Confirm in writing:
• trade date / settlement date
• exact dollar amount and specific positions/shares transferred
• receiving account number

If your plan supports in-plan Roth only:
This is an in-plan Roth conversion inside my [401(k)/403(b)]. Keep payroll deferrals as pre-tax.

Custodian — set RMD/QCD cadence (and safe-harbor help)
Set my RMD from account ending [xxxx] to distribute $[annual amount] [monthly/quarterly], with [__% federal / __% state] withholding starting [mm/dd]. Please confirm schedule, withholding percentages, and first payment date. Also process a Qualified Charitable Distribution of $[amount] from my IRA directly to: [Charity legal name], EIN [xx-xxxxxxx], [mailing address]. Email written confirmations for both the RMD setup and QCD.

Optional line if catching up withholding late in the year:
Increase federal withholding on remaining RMD payments to __% to ensure safe-harbor coverage for 2025.

Quick send-list (so you don't forget)

- ☐ CPA email (attach Action Sheet + last 1040 + YTD income)
- ☐ Custodian conversion instruction (in-kind, 0% withholding)
- ☐ Custodian RMD cadence + withholding (and QCD, if applicable)

Filing checklist (after confirmations)

- ☐ Conversion confirmation (amount, date, positions)
- ☐ RMD schedule letter (cadence, withholding)
- ☐ QCD confirmation + charity acknowledgment letter
- ☐ Calendar holds created: **Mid-Year**, **Nov/Dec True-Up**, **Annual Legacy Check**
- ☐ Action Sheet printed (v___, date-stamped) and saved to digital vault

Tip: Use a consistent filename and versioning scheme: ActionSheet_[LastName]_v03_2025-08-17.pdf — and keep the latest copy at the front of your binder and in your password manager/vault.

Tools & Printables You'll Use

1) One-Page Action Sheet (above)
Purpose: your single source of truth for this year's numbers, dates, and guardrails.
When to use: fill once now; update at Mid-Year and Nov/Dec True-Up.
Pro tip: version/date it every change (v03, 2025-08-17). Keep one printed on your binder and one PDF in your vault.
What "good" looks like:

- Planned conversion = **Headroom − $2k–$5k buffer**
- IRMAA buffer ≥ **$1k–$5k** after the conversion
- Conversion **in-kind**, **0% withholding**, tax paid from cash
- If RMD year: **RMD → (QCD) → conversion** sequence set, with cadence + withholding that meets **safe harbor**

2) Tax Bracket Filler Planner (Pillar 3)

Purpose: size conversions precisely per year without crossing tax or IRMAA cliffs.

When to use: at setup, then each Mid-Year and Nov/Dec. Also use after a market dip.

Item	Value / Notes
Year	20__
Filing status	_______
Target bracket (%)	__%
Top-of-bracket ($)	________
Projected taxable income ($)	__________
IRMAA next tier (MAGI) ($)	__________
Headroom (Top − Projected) ($)	__________
Desired buffer — Bracket	$2k–$5k
Desired buffer — IRMAA	$1k–$5k
Planned conversion this year ($)	__________ *(in-kind, 0% withholding)*
IRMAA buffer AFTER conversion ($)	__________ *(≥ $1k–$5k?)*

Notes (offsets: DAF/loss harvest/medical/HSA, SS/RMD timing, fund distributions): ____

Multi-year ladder (3–5 yrs):

Year	Bridge year?	Target bracket	Planned conversion	IRMAA buffer	Offsets	Notes (SS/RMD)
20__	☐	__%	$________	$________	______	______________
20__	☐	__%	$________	$________	______	______________

3) RMD-Year Checklist & Withholding Safe-Harbor Tracker (Pillar 4)

Purpose: put required income on rails and avoid penalties or IRMAA surprises.

RMD-Year Checklist (one page):

Sequencing

☐ IRA QCD(s) first (age 70½+) – $_______ (direct IRA→charity; ack letters saved)

☐ Remaining RMD satisfied – $_______

Cadence: ☐ Monthly ☐ Quarterly Start: __/__/__

☐ Post-RMD Roth conversion (only if buffers allow) – $_______

In-kind, 0% withholding Cliff checks

☐ Bracket buffer left ≥ $2k–$5k

☐ IRMAA buffer left ≥ $1k–$5k (2-yr lookback)

☐ Social Security taxation impact reviewed

☐ Taxable fund capital-gains distributions checked (often Dec) Paper & Proof

☐ RMD/QCD confirmations saved ☐ 1099-R (and QCD letters) filed later

Safe-Harbor Tracker (math box):

Item	Value / Notes
Prior-year total tax (1040 line 24)	$________
Safe harbor target	☐ 100% ☐ 110% (> $150k PY AGI) = $________
This-year 90% of projected tax (optional)	$________
YTD withholding	$________
Estimated payments	$________
Gap	$________
Plan	Increase RMD withholding to **Fed** __% **/ State** __% **OR** pay estimate on __ **/**___**/20**___.

(Remember: late year RMD withholding is treated as paid evenly all year.)

4) Legacy Brief & Beneficiary Map (Pillar 5)

Purpose: make inheritance fast, clean, and tax-smart.

Beneficiary Map (snapshot):

Account Type (Roth/Pre-tax/Taxable/HSA)	Primary %	Contingent %	Per stirpes?	EIN (charity)
	______%	______%	☐ Yes ☐ No	
	______%	______%	☐ Yes ☐ No	
	______%	______%	☐ Yes ☐ No	
	______%	______%	☐ Yes ☐ No	

Notes (Roth start yr, TOD/POD)

Legacy Brief (1–2 pages):

- **Contacts:** Advisor, CPA, Attorney, custodian phone numbers
- **Account list:** who inherits what (%), **Roth earliest open year**
- **First 30–60 days:** open inherited IRA/Roth; confirm basis step-up on taxable; gather 1099-R/5498 later
- **10-year rule summary:** non-spouse must empty by 12/31 of year 10; spouse options listed
- **Location & access:** where originals live; digital vault instructions

Update cadence: annually (birthday month) and after life events.

5) Market-Dip Trigger Card

Purpose: act decisively during volatility without blowing past buffers.

MARKET-DIP TRIGGER CARD

Trigger definition "If portfolio declines by ___% from the recent high (as tracked in [app/spreadsheet]), and my remaining bracket headroom is ≥ $________ and IRMAA buffer ≥ $________,

THEN convert up to $________ (not exceeding remaining headroom), in-kind, 0% withholding."

Guardrails

☐ Re-compute headroom before executing

☐ Leave ≥ $2k–$5k under bracket top and ≥ $1k–$5k under IRMAA tier

☐ If RMD year: confirm RMD (and any QCD) already satisfied Execution notes

- Account to convert from: __________
- Positions to move in-kind: __________
- Custodian confirmation requested: date/amount/shares

How to measure the trigger: use your portfolio value high watermark (or a simple index proxy you track consistently), then calculate percentage drop.

Print-Ready Bundle (how to package)

- **Front:** One-Page **Action Sheet** (latest version + date)
- **Tab A: Tax Bracket Filler Planner** (current year + ladder)
- **Tab B: RMD-Year Checklist + Safe-Harbor Tracker**
- **Tab C: Legacy Brief + Beneficiary Map** + confirmations
- **Back pocket:** Copy of CPA/custodian **confirmations** and last **1040** summary

File naming (digital):
ActionSheet_[LastName]_v03_2025-08-17.pdf (mirror for each tool).
Security: store PDFs in your password manager/digital vault; share **location + access** with executor and one backup.

Real-World Micro Example (illustrative)

Numbers are directional and rounded. Swap in your own bracket tops, IRMAA tier, and state rate.

Snapshot

- **Headroom (22% lane): $41,000**
- **Planned conversion: $38,000** (leaves ≈ **$3,000** bracket buffer)
- **RMD: None yet** (pre-RMD "bridge" year)
- **Market-dip trigger: −12%** → convert **up to $6,000** more (only if buffers remain)
- **Calendar holds: Mid-Year 6/15**, **True-Up 11/20**, **Annual Legacy Check** (birthday month)
- **Execution:** Custodian converts **in-kind**, **0% withholding**; CPA confirms **safe harbor** is covered

Mini-Math (how the dollars work)

1) Bracket math (illustrative):

- Headroom = **$41,000**
- Planned conversion = **$38,000**
- **Buffer left = $41,000 − $38,000 = $3,000**

2) Federal tax cash you'll need:

- On $38,000 at 22% → **$8,360**

    - Calculation: 38,000 × 0.22 = **8,360**
- If the −12% trigger hits and you add **$6,000**:
    - Extra tax at 22% → **$1,320** (6,000 × 0.22 = 1,320)
- **Total cash set aside for federal** (conversion + top-off) → **$8,360 + $1,320 = $9,680**
    - Step-by-step: 8,360 + 1,320 = **9,680**
      (Add state tax if applicable.)

3) Future RMD "shrink" (directional):

- Total moved to Roth (if trigger used) = **$38,000 + $6,000 = $44,000**
    - 38,000 + 6,000 = **44,000**
- Early-year RMD rate ≈ **4%** (illustrative)
- First-year RMD reduction ≈ **$44,000 × 0.04 = $1,760**
    - 1% of 44,000 = 440; 4 × 440 = **1,760**

IRMAA guardrail (quick check)

- **IRMAA next tier (MAGI):** $________
- **Your MAGI after $38k conversion:** $________
- **Buffer left:** $________ (target **$1k–$5k**).
- If the market-dip top-off would pierce the tier, **skip the top-off**.

What you actually do (timeline)

This week

1. **Fill the Action Sheet** with the numbers above.
2. **Email CPA** (true-up & safe-harbor): "Planned $38k conversion (buffer ~$3k); confirm IRMAA margin and withholding sufficiency."
3. **Message custodian**: "Convert **$38,000 in-kind** from Traditional to Roth; **0% withholding**; written confirmation of date/positions."
4. **Set calendar holds**: 6/15, 11/20, birthday-month legacy check.

If market drops −12% later

- Re-check headroom & IRMAA buffer.
- If safe, instruct **additional $6,000 in-kind** conversion (0% withholding).
- Note added **$1,320** federal tax cash needed.

Year-end (11/20 True-Up)

- CPA confirms **remaining safe headroom** and **IRMAA**.
- Optional **small top-off** conversion if buffers remain.
- Verify no surprise capital-gain distributions will nudge you over.

Paperwork you'll see

- **1099-R** (reports distribution/convert) and **5498** (Roth funding) next year—file with your **Action Sheet**.
- Custodian **conversion confirmation** (amount/date/positions) and any **RMD/QCD** confirmations (if applicable).

Why this works

- You **act now** (not perfectly later), staying **inside the bracket** and **under IRMAA**.
- You keep every converted dollar **invested** (in-kind, 0% withholding) and pay tax from cash.
- You reduce future **RMDs**, add **tax-free optionality** in Roth, and run the year on **three simple dates**.

Action Step (what to complete now)

Goal: walk away with a dated, dollar-specific plan you can run without second-guessing.

1) Fill the Action Sheet (amounts, dates, buffers)

- **Compute headroom:** Top-of-bracket − Projected taxable = Headroom.
- **Set your conversion:** Headroom − $2k–$5k buffer = Planned conversion $_____.
- **IRMAA check:** Confirm you're **$1k–$5k** under the next tier **after** the conversion.
- **Execution window: __ /___/20___ → __ /___/20___** (pick a real week on your calendar).
- **Market-dip trigger:** "If portfolio −%, **convert up to** **$___** (still within buffers)."
- **RMD/QCD block:** If RMD year, record **amount, cadence, start date, withholding**; add **QCD $_____** (70½+) and month.

2) Send the CPA & custodian messages

- **CPA (true-up):** Bracket top, projected taxable, headroom, **planned conversion + buffers**, IRMAA margin, RMD cadence/withholding, QCD amount/timing, and **safe-harbor** status.
- **Custodian/Plan (conversion):** "Convert **$_____ in-kind**, **0% withholding**; confirm date and positions in writing."
- **Custodian (RMD/QCD):** "Set RMD **$_____** ☐M/☐Q with **Fed __% / State __%**; process **QCD $_____** to [Charity, EIN]; send confirmations."

3) Create the 3 calendar holds (make them recurring)

- **Mid-Year Review (May/June):** Update income; re-size headroom; adjust withholding/RMD/QCD; reconfirm IRMAA buffer.
- **Nov/Dec True-Up:** Ask CPA for **remaining safe headroom**; consider small top-off conversion **before 12/31**.
- **Annual Legacy Check (birthday month):** Verify beneficiaries/TOD, Roth 5-year clock noted, Legacy Brief location shared.

4) Print & file (and save a PDF)

- **Print** the Action Sheet (v__ + date) and place it on top of your binder.
- **Save** a PDF copy to your vault/password manager (e.g., ActionSheet_[LastName]_v01_YYYY-MM-DD.pdf).
- **Attach** custodian & CPA confirmations when they arrive (conversion, RMD setup, QCD acknowledgment).

5) 5-Minute Sanity Pass (go/no-go before executing)

- ☐ **Bracket buffer** ≥ $2k and **IRMAA buffer** ≥ $1k after conversion
- ☐ **Sequence** correct in RMD years: **RMD → (QCD) → Conversion**
- ☐ **Conversion** is **in-kind** with **0% withholding**; tax will be paid from cash
- ☐ If IRA **basis** exists, Form 8606 on file / basis isolation plan noted
- ☐ **Roth earliest open year** recorded (≥5 tax years or clock started)
- ☐ Dates on your calendar match the Action Sheet

Deliverable (today)

A **dated, dollar-specific plan** you can execute confidently—**bracket-safe, IRMAA-aware, and legacy-ready.**

(Educational only – coordinate specifics with your CPA/attorney.)

Pillar 6 — Executive Summary

Readiness Snapshot (60-second check)

- Know your **target bracket** (22%/24%) and **IRMAA buffer** (keep $1k–$5k under next tier).
- Calculate **headroom** (top-of-bracket − projected taxable) and set a **planned conversion** (headroom − $2k–$5k buffer).
- Confirm **RMD status** (not started / start year / in progress with cadence & withholding).

The 15-Minute Plan (minute-by-minute)

- **0–3:** Pull numbers → top-of-bracket, projected taxable, headroom, buffered conversion, IRMAA buffer after move.
- **4–6:** Decide mechanics → account to convert from, **in-kind** method, **0% withholding**, set **market-dip trigger** (e.g., −10%/−15%).
- **7–9:** Put RMD/QCD on rails → RMD amount, **monthly/quarterly** cadence, withholding to meet **safe harbor**, QCD (70½+) plan.
- **10–12:** Legacy quick pass → verify **beneficiaries/TOD**, Roth **5-year clock**, update **Legacy Brief**.
- **13–15: Send & schedule** → email CPA, message custodian/plan, add 3 calendar holds (Mid-Year, Nov/Dec True-Up, Annual Legacy Check).

One-Page Action Sheet (fill now; print)

- Captures: **bracket plan**, **conversion details** (in-kind, 0% WH, window, dip trigger), **RMD/QCD/withholding**, **legacy checks**, and **contacts**.
- Version/date it; keep printed on your binder and saved to your vault.

Tools & Printables You'll Use

- **Action Sheet** (this year's control panel).
- **Tax Bracket Filler Planner** (size conversions, multi-year ladder).
- **RMD-Year Checklist & Safe-Harbor Tracker** (sequencing + penalty avoidance).
- **Legacy Brief & Beneficiary Map** (clean inheritance).
- **Market-Dip Trigger Card** (pre-written rule to top-off during volatility).

Real-World Micro Example (illustrative)

- Headroom **$41k** in 22% → convert **$38k** (≈$3k buffer).
- **No RMD**; set **−12%** market trigger to add **$6k** if safe.
- Calendar holds: **6/15** Mid-Year, **11/20** True-Up, **birthday month** Legacy Check.
- CPA confirms **safe harbor**; custodian executes **in-kind, 0% withholding**.

Action Step (what to complete now)

1. **Fill the Action Sheet** (amounts, dates, buffers).
2. **Email CPA** (bracket/IRMAA/safe-harbor true-up) and **message custodian/plan** (conversion + RMD/QCD).
3. **Create 3 calendar holds** (Mid-Year, True-Up, Legacy).
4. **Print & file** the sheet on top of your binder; save a PDF copy.

Outcome: A dated, dollar-specific plan you can execute confidently—**bracket-safe, IRMAA-aware, and legacy-ready.** *(Educational only – coordinate specifics with your CPA/attorney.)*

Conclusion: Your Roadmap Starts Now

If this book has made one thing clear, it's this: a tax-smart retirement isn't luck—it's a sequence of simple, repeatable decisions. You now have the playbook to move money from "tax-later and tax-unknown" to **tax-free and under your control**: use a multi-year Roth conversion plan, fill brackets (not emotions), watch IRMAA tiers, and let guaranteed income tools and smart cashflow design reduce sequence-of-returns risk.

Markets will move. Tax laws may change. But a process built on math, milestones, and checklists keeps you from guessing—and from paying more than you need to.

What to Carry Forward

- **Taxes are a risk you can price.** Use **top-of-bracket** conversions and keep a **headroom buffer** so you don't spill into higher brackets or IRMAA tiers.
- **Roth is optionality.** Tax-free growth, no lifetime RMDs, and cleaner estate transfers give you flexibility when markets wobble or expenses spike.
- **Process beats prediction.** Calendars, scripts, one-page sheets, and a 15-minute review cadence turn strategy into action.

Your Next 15 Minutes (do this today)

1. Open your **One-Page Action Sheet** and write your target **conversion bracket** and **IRMAA buffer**.
2. Add **three calendar holds**: mid-year check, year-end true-up, and a brief CPA touchpoint.
3. Send the prewritten **CPA and custodian messages** (appendix) so everyone is aligned on in-kind transfers and withholding.
4. Create a **Tax Folder** (digital/physical) with tabs for **1099-R, 5498, QCD acknowledgments, and confirmations**.

The Next 90 Days

- **Size the conversion.** Use your projected AGI, deductions, and headroom to right-size this year's amount.
- **Choose funding & mechanics.** Prefer **in-kind** conversions to stay invested; keep **0% withholding** on the conversion and satisfy taxes via RMD withholding or quarterly estimates to preserve tax-free capital.
- **Stage the execution.** Consider **two or three tranches** with a market-dip trigger (if your plan calls for it).
- **Document everything.** Save confirmations; update your worksheet; note any QCD/DAF coordination.
- **Review with your CPA.** Confirm interactions across Social Security, Medicare, and state taxes.

Your Annual Cadence (set it and keep it)

- **Spring:** Project income, update headroom, confirm IRMAA look-back implications.
- **Summer:** Mid-year check; deploy a second tranche if needed.

- **Fall:** Decide on **QCDs/DAF** timing; revisit medical deductions, SALT, and itemizing vs. standard deduction.
- **December: True-up conversion** to the top of your bracket; use year-end withholding if needed to meet safe harbor.
- **January–May:** Reconcile **1099-R** and **5498**, file **Form 8606** if applicable, and archive everything in your Tax Folder.

Guardrails to Respect

- **No recharacterization of conversions.** Double-check amounts before you click "submit."
- **Pro-rata rule applies** across all traditional IRAs; isolate basis where appropriate.
- **Sequence matters in RMD years:** take the RMD first, then convert.
- **Protect your buffers:** keep a few thousand dollars of cushion below your bracket cap and IRMAA tier to avoid surprises.
- **Laws evolve.** Many individual tax provisions are scheduled to change after 2025 unless Congress acts; your multi-year ladder lets you adapt without panic.

A Final Word

Retirement should feel like **freedom**, not a tug-of-war with the tax code. You've organized your numbers, chosen a bracket, planned for healthcare thresholds, and built a glidepath that doesn't depend on perfect market timing. Keep the plan simple. Keep the calendar dates. Keep your documents tidy. Then enjoy your life—confident that more of what you earned will stay with you and the people you love.

If you'd like help implementing this plan or pressure-testing your headroom and IRMAA buffers, schedule a brief **Retirement Tax Strategy Review**. A 20-minute check with a specialist can save hours of research—and potentially years of unnecessary taxes.

To a calm, tax-free retirement—on your terms.

Appendix

- **Appendix A:** 15-Minute Tax-Free Action Sheet (fillable).
- **Appendix B:** CPA & Custodian Email/Scripts.
- **Appendix C:** Quick-Reference Tables (RMD, IRMAA, bracket headroom worksheet).
- **Appendix D:** Sample Forms (1099-R, 5498, 8606) with notes.
- **Appendix E:** Tool Links & Spreadsheet Instructions (calculator, trackers).

Glossary of Terms

1099-R (Form 1099-R)
Tax form reporting distributions and conversions from pensions, annuities, IRAs, and employer plans. Keep every 1099-R for your tax file. *See also:* 5498, Withholding.
5498 (Form 5498)
Year-end tax form your custodian issues to report IRA contributions and Roth conversions received. It's informational; you don't file it with your return. *See also:* 1099-R.
8606 (Form 8606)
Tax form that tracks after-tax (nondeductible) IRA basis and reports taxable vs. nontaxable portions of conversions. *See also:* Basis, Pro-Rata Rule.
401(k)/403(b)/457(b)
Employer retirement plans. May allow **in-plan Roth conversions (IRR)** and rollovers to IRAs. Rules and fees vary by plan. *See also:* In-Plan Roth Conversion, Rollover.
Adjusted Gross Income (AGI)
Your gross income minus allowable adjustments, before standard or itemized deductions. A starting point for many tax thresholds. *See also:* MAGI, Taxable Income.
Age Milestones
Key ages for planning: **59½** (10% penalty on early IRA withdrawals ends), **65** (Medicare eligibility), **70½** (QCD eligibility), **73/75** (RMD start, depending on birth year). *See also:* QCD, RMD.
Annual Conversion Ladder
A multi-year plan to convert portions of pre-tax accounts to Roth, targeting the top of a chosen tax bracket each year to control taxes and IRMAA. *See also:* Bracket Filling, Headroom.
Annuity, Fixed Indexed (FIA)
An insurance contract that credits interest based on an index (e.g., S&P 500) with protections against market loss, subject to caps/participation rates/spreads. Often used to create guaranteed lifetime income or as a volatility buffer. *See also:* GLWB, Participation Rate, Cap, Spread.
Basis (IRA Basis)
After-tax money in an IRA from nondeductible contributions. Basis is not taxed again when withdrawn or converted, but it's subject to the **Pro-Rata Rule** across all your IRAs. *See also:* 8606, Pro-Rata Rule.

Beneficiary (IRA/Roth)
The person(s) or entity named to receive your account at death. Post-SECURE Act, most non-spouse beneficiaries must empty inherited accounts within 10 years. *See also:* Inherited IRA, Roth for Heirs.
Bracket (Tax Bracket)
The tax rate that applies to your last dollar of ordinary income. Planning often targets the **top of a chosen bracket** (e.g., 22%/24%) to "fill" headroom efficiently. *See also:* Headroom, Marginal vs. Effective Rate.
Bracket Filling (Top-of-Bracket Strategy)
Converting just enough each year to reach—but not exceed—the top of your target bracket, giving you predictable tax costs and IRMAA control. *See also:* Headroom, IRMAA.
Cap / Participation Rate / Spread (FIA Terms)
Crediting method details for FIAs: a **cap** limits credited interest, a **participation rate** credits a percentage of index gains, and a **spread** subtracts a fixed percentage from gains. *See also:* Fixed Indexed Annuity.
Conversion (Roth Conversion)
Moving money from a pre-tax account (IRA/401k) into a Roth account. The converted amount is taxable as ordinary income in the year of conversion. *See also:* Five-Year Rule (Conversions), Recharacterization (not allowed).
Custodian
Financial institution holding your IRA/retirement assets and issuing required tax forms (1099-R/5498). *See also:* 1099-R, 5498.
DAF (Donor-Advised Fund)
A charitable account that lets you "bunch" deductions in high-income years. Not eligible for QCDs. *See also:* Charitable Bunching, QCD.
Estimated Taxes / Safe Harbor
Quarterly payments to avoid penalties. "Safe harbor" generally means paying 100% (110% for higher incomes) of last year's total tax or 90% of the current year's. *See also:* Withholding.
Effective Tax Rate
Your total tax divided by total income—an average rate. Useful for big-picture planning, but **marginal rate** drives the cost of conversions. *See also:* Marginal Tax Rate.
Five-Year Rule (Roth IRA & Conversions)
Two clocks: (1) **Roth IRA** must be open 5 tax years and you must be 59½ (or meet another exception) for **qualified** tax-free earnings; (2) **Each conversion** has its own 5-year penalty clock for early withdrawals of converted principal if under 59½. *See also:* Qualified Distribution.

GLWB (Guaranteed Lifetime Withdrawal Benefit)
An annuity rider that provides a minimum lifetime income stream regardless of market performance, subject to terms and fees. *See also:* Fixed Indexed Annuity.
Headroom (Bracket Headroom)
The dollar gap between your projected taxable income and the top of your target tax bracket (or an IRMAA tier). Guides how much to convert without spilling over. *See also:* Bracket Filling, IRMAA.
HSA (Health Savings Account)
Triple tax advantage: deductible contributions, tax-free growth, and tax-free withdrawals for qualified medical expenses. Can be used strategically in conversion years. *See also:* MAGI, Medicare.
Inherited IRA / Roth IRA
Accounts received from a decedent. Most non-spouse beneficiaries must fully distribute within 10 years; spouses have additional options. *See also:* Beneficiary, Roth for Heirs.
In-Kind Conversion
Converting securities "as is" instead of selling to cash first, preserving market exposure during the conversion. *See also:* Roth Conversion.
In-Plan Roth Conversion (IRR)
Converting within a 401(k)/403(b) from pre-tax to the plan's Roth source. Different from rolling to a Roth IRA; plan rules and 5-year nuances apply. *See also:* Roth 401(k), Five-Year Rule.
IRMAA (Income-Related Monthly Adjustment Amount)
Medicare Part B and D premium surcharges based on **MAGI** from two years prior. Planning uses buffers to avoid crossing tiers unnecessarily. *See also:* MAGI, Medicare.
Ladder (Conversion Ladder)
A scheduled, multi-year series of conversions designed to use low-tax "bridge years" and manage IRMAA tiers. *See also:* Bridge Years, Headroom.
MAGI (Modified Adjusted Gross Income)
AGI plus certain add-backs (e.g., tax-exempt interest). Used to determine IRMAA tiers and some credit/deduction eligibility. *See also:* AGI, IRMAA.
Marginal Tax Rate
The rate applied to your next dollar of ordinary income—the key rate for conversion decisions. *See also:* Effective Tax Rate, Bracket.
Market-Value Adjustment (MVA)
An annuity provision that can adjust surrender values up or down based on interest rate movements when you withdraw beyond free amounts. *See also:* Surrender Charge, Fixed Indexed Annuity.

Medicare (Parts A, B, D)
Federal health insurance (generally starts at 65). Part B/D premiums are subject to **IRMAA** based on MAGI with a two-year lookback. *See also:* IRMAA, MAGI.
Mega Backdoor Roth
After-tax contributions to a 401(k) plus in-plan Roth conversion or in-service rollover to a Roth IRA, allowing very large Roth funding when a plan permits. *See also:* Backdoor Roth, In-Plan Roth Conversion.
Qualified Charitable Distribution (QCD)
Direct transfer from an IRA to a qualified charity for those **70½+**. Counts toward IRA RMD and reduces MAGI; not allowed to DAFs or private foundations. *See also:* RMD, MAGI, DAF.
Qualified Distribution (Roth)
A Roth IRA withdrawal that is tax-free: account open 5 tax years **and** you're 59½ (or meet an exception such as death, disability, first-home up to limits). *See also:* Five-Year Rule.
Recharacterization (Conversions)
Undoing a Roth conversion—**no longer allowed** for conversions completed after 2017. (You can still recharacterize current-year contributions.) *See also:* Roth Contribution.
Required Beginning Date (RBD)
The deadline to start RMDs from traditional accounts (generally April 1 following the year you reach your applicable RMD age). *See also:* RMD.
Required Minimum Distribution (RMD)
The minimum annual withdrawal required from most pre-tax retirement accounts starting at age **73 or 75** (depending on birth year). Roth IRAs owned by you have no lifetime RMDs. *See also:* RBD, Roth for Heirs.
Roth 401(k) vs. Roth IRA
Both grow tax-free; Roth 401(k)s may still have plan-level RMDs (often avoided by rolling to a Roth IRA). Roth IRAs offer broader investment/control. *See also:* In-Plan Roth Conversion, RMD.
Roth Contribution (Annual)
Regular yearly additions to a Roth account, subject to income and plan limits. Distinct from **conversions** and can be recharacterized within deadlines. *See also:* Roth Conversion.
Roth Conversion "Backdoor"
Two-step method: make a nondeductible traditional IRA contribution, then convert to Roth. The **Pro-Rata Rule** applies across all IRAs, so isolating basis may be needed. *See also:* Basis, 8606, Pro-Rata Rule.

Roth for Heirs (Estate Use)
Leaving Roth assets can provide tax-free withdrawals to beneficiaries (subject to the 10-year rule for most). *See also:* Beneficiary, Inherited IRA.
SALT (State and Local Taxes)
Itemized deduction for state and local taxes, currently capped for federal purposes. Interacts with your decision to itemize vs. take the standard deduction. *See also:* Deductions.
Sequence-of-Returns Risk
The order of market returns matters when withdrawing; early losses can harm portfolios. Roth assets and FIAs can act as buffers in down markets. *See also:* Fixed Indexed Annuity.
Standard vs. Itemized Deduction
Two ways to reduce taxable income. Choosing correctly can create more room ("headroom") for Roth conversions in a given year. *See also:* Headroom, SALT.
Surrender Charge (Annuities)
A fee for taking out more than the free-withdrawal amount during the surrender period. Know your schedule before withdrawals or conversions. *See also:* Market-Value Adjustment.
Taxable Income
AGI minus deductions (standard or itemized). Determines your tax bracket and how much headroom remains for conversions. *See also:* AGI, Bracket.
TCJA (Tax Cuts and Jobs Act) Sunset
Most individual rate cuts are scheduled to expire after 2025 absent new law, which can make pre-2026 conversions more attractive for some. *See also:* Bracket, Headroom.
Uniform Lifetime Table
IRS table used to calculate RMDs for account owners (not beneficiaries). The first-year divisor gives a ballpark percentage to withdraw. *See also:* RMD.
Volatility Buffer
Assets or strategies (e.g., Roth funds, FIAs) used to avoid selling investments at a loss during down markets. *See also:* Sequence-of-Returns Risk.
Withholding (vs. Estimated Payments)
Taxes taken out at the source (e.g., from RMDs) count as if paid evenly all year, which can help with penalties. Many planners set **0% withholding on conversions** and withhold from RMDs or do a year-end "catch-up." *See also:* Safe Harbor, 1099-R.

Note: This glossary is educational and not tax, legal, or investment advice. If you want, I can reformat this into a two-column Word table or add any company-specific annuity riders/terms you use.

Made in United States
North Haven, CT
10 November 2026

22097463R00100